Psycho-Oncology: Psychological Assessment for Cancer Patients

Terminal Illness-Psychotherapy-Quality of Life

Authors

Suantak Demkhosei Vaiphei & Fariza Saidin

Product details

ASIN: B0D9227N5J

Publisher: Notion Press (8 July 2024)

Language: English

ISBN-13: 979-8894758664

Country of Origin: India

Why This Book?

To highlight the emerging needs of palliative end-of-life care in Indian clinical settings.

The book focuses on delivering a good/meaningful death and dying process, which becomes the underlying factor in the formation of the current research book.

Palliative care practitioners may seize the opportunity to encourage patients to find meaning in suffering as they face inevitable death.

The meaning-making process can be generative for patients' feelings of anxiety, guilt, or hopelessness that seem punishing and unrelenting at the end of life and can be transformed into ways of actively exploring the relationship with self and others.

Finding meaning at the end of life is no small endeavour: it takes courage, commitment, and conviction to reflect upon and take ownership of one's existence.

The value of Spiritual psychotherapy in end-of-life care is that it encourages patients to seriously explore their past, present, and future in terms of meaningful choices and the experiences that created and continue to generate their stories.

Helping patients explore the "why" of their existence "Why am I here?" and the meaning of their lives "Did my life matter?", Spiritual psychotherapy offers dying patients a way to bear the burden of their suffering and eventual death with strength, and dignity

For cancer patients, the domains of quality care include receiving adequate treatment for pain and symptom control, avoiding inappropriate prolongation of dying, achieving a sense of spiritual peace, relieving burdens, and strengthening relationships with loved ones. Clearly, for both patient and physician, spirituality issues are essential elements of quality palliative care.

It could serve as a reference book for students and scholars interested in exploring the psycho-oncological issues in higher education and research.

CONTENTS

Preface

Psycho-oncology, which deals with the importance of understanding psychological issues in terminal ill diagnosis began in the 1950s and the mid-1970s. In developed countries, the stigma attached to terminal illness diminished in the 20th century. However, the Indian attitude towards mental health issues associated with cancer is still a long-standing stigma. The existing stigma attached to cancer and mental illness constituted major barriers to the optimal psychosocial care of patients and loved ones. The crucial to understand society's attitudes toward mental illness associated with cancer hugely impact patients' quality of life and wellbeing. The psycho-social ramifications are serious, long-lasting, and broad and affect patients in all stages of cancer. Negative affectivity and social stress activate the sympathetic nervous system, the hypothalamus-pituitary-adrenal axis, which affects the immune system involved in inflammation. In India, Psycho-oncology is a dormant area with scanty research availability. The healthcare system in India caring for cancer does not make psycho-social aspects an essential part of their assessment, focusing mainly on the physical pain symptoms. The book analyzed various psychosocial factors affecting cancer patients in rural India and identified assessment tools that play an important role in its management. It highlights those factors impeding the incorporation of psychological knowledge in clinical care and a new horizon in Indian palliative end-of-life care.

The practice and research on psycho-oncology in India are not well known, though some research has been going on for years. Either readers are not aware of the publications or do not have access to such literature. This handbook attempts to share the practice of psycho-oncology from an Indian perspective. This book thus provides a resource book on psycho-oncology from an Indian perspective and provides information about Indian research and literature. This is not a textbook but should help clinicians and researchers looking after cancer patients and their families. The book is a short introductory book and not a comprehensive one, for which the readers should look for more voluminous and detailed books. This book is a pragmatic one and simplifies this complex field for clinicians and researchers. Doctors, nurses, psychologists, social workers, and others involved in cancer care would find this book useful.

Dr. Suantak Demkhosei Vaiphei
Ph.D. Psychology

Prologue

Cancer, and its modern scientific medical treatments, have led to the improvement of general living conditions, and an increase in life expectancy has led to increasing the general prevalence of a long-standing oncologic disease with a variety of physical and psychosocial problems. Psychosocial issues usually modulate the course of the disease, which mainly has a deep impact on the patient's physical and mental well-being. The long-standing psycho-oncologic symptoms range from physical pain, fatigue, and loss of autonomous life to anxiety, depression, and strain on personal relationships and have a deep impact on quality of life. As a result, the demand for psychosocial interventions to treat and support patients with cancer disease and cancer survivors has dramatically increased over the last decades. Psycho-oncology has risen as a relatively new interdisciplinary field to address these issues and provide support for patients confronting numerous challenges throughout the different stages of the disease.

Since the 1970s, psycho-oncology has developed into a firmly established part of oncological care in several developed countries. However, it remains an unheard area of care in Indian clinical practices. Existing psychologically distressing symptoms, especially depression, stress, and anxiety lead to a poorer prognosis for cancer disease and higher mortality risk. Theoretically, the scope for cancer prevention & treatment effectiveness of early detection has been well recognized by Indian clinicians. The term psycho-oncology refers to "diverse psychological, social, behavioral and psychiatric issues related to cancer prevention, cancer illness, and treatment and cancer survivorship." Psycho-oncology refers to psychological, social, and behavioural issues related to cancer prevention, treatment, and survivorship. At present, cancer in India is around 2.25 million with 1.1 million new cases per year. The primary concern of Psycho-oncology deals with the emotional responses of patients and loved ones, and factors influencing cancer morbidity and mortality. Several existing research highlight that psycho-social factors increase the rate at which cancer worsens leading to mortality.

The psycho-social ramifications are serious, long-lasting, and broad and affect patients in all stages of cancer. Negative affectivity and social stress activate the sympathetic nervous system, the hypothalamus-pituitary-adrenal axis, which affects the immune system involved in inflammation. In India, Psycho-oncology is a dormant area with scanty research availability. The healthcare system in India caring for cancer does not make psycho-social aspects an essential part of their assessment, focusing mainly on the physical pain symptoms. The present report analyzed various psychosocial factors affecting cancer patients in rural India and identified assessment tools that play an important role in its management.

Psycho-oncology is a relatively new medical field that was developed to investigate the most neglected issues in oncological research, which are the impact of behavioral and psychosocial factors on cancer morbidity and mortality and the psychological influence of cancer on patients, their loved ones, and clinicians. The psycho-oncological research is a multidisciplinary subdiscipline of cancer care that encompasses assessing anxiety, fear of cancer recurrence, depression, trauma, distress, cognitive function, fatigue, sexual function and intimacy, and sleep disturbance. The existing psychosocial issues in terminal ill experience are not limited to cancer patients but also to their families, loved ones, clinicians, and caregivers. The psycho-oncological interventions are effective in dealing with the destigmatization of cancer and mental disease, change in relationships, and change in focus from increasing survival and life expectancy to improving quality of life and development of palliative end-of-life care. Cancer unlike any other disease demands a greater amount of appropriate care toward psychologically distressing symptoms.

Psychosocial oncology is coming of age. While the survival rates of cancer patients have increased, many patients suffer from treatment-related long-lasting effects that may adversely affect their mental health and health-related quality of life. Along with the changes in therapeutic strategies, physicians should pay more attention to the psychosocial problems secondary to cancer as it is well-recognized that the diagnosis of cancer and its treatment can be extremely stressful and emotional for cancer patients. Psychosocial oncology refers to the multidisciplinary subdiscipline of cancer care created to improve patients' mental well-being by offering strategies to help them cope with the demands of treatment and uncertainty of disease outcomes in the best possible way. Psychosocial care should be available before diagnosis beyond palliative care and survival. The most common prevailing psychiatric symptoms patients with cancer experience are adjustment disorders, major depression, delirium, and unwanted risky behaviors. The cancer's physical pain symptoms are closely associated with the patient's psychological functioning, which requires trained professionals to deliver pain and non-pain symptoms management. The current challenges in cancer diagnosis are visible in cancer survivors suffering from treatment-related long-lasting effects that may adversely affect patient mental health and health-related quality of life. Clinicians are required to shift their attention and acknowledge the psychosocial problems secondary to cancer diagnosis are extremely stressful and emotional for cancer patients. The core of psycho-oncological assessment is to help patients cope with the demands of treatment and uncertainty of disease outcomes in the best possible way. It aims to provide quality psychosocial care beyond palliative care and survival before diagnosis. Psychosocial assessment should be recognized as a universal human right, and quality cancer care must integrate the psychosocial domain into routine care.

CHAPTER – ONE

Cancer: A Major Public Health Concern in India

Abstract

The underlying aim of the study is to investigate the underlying reasons behind the rapid growth of cancer populations and the cancer mortality rates in present India. The study emphasizes cancerous factors, the underlying barriers behind the unfruitfulness of the terminal diagnosis, and the proposed solutions or preventive measures in traditional ways. The current study is an analytical study on the collected data and reports from the following reliable sources:

- The Population-Based Cancer Registries Data' of the Central and State Governments.
- The Data from the National Cancer Registry and Regional Cancer Centers.
- National Family Health Survey of India (NFHS-3), NICPR-National Institute of Cancer Prevention and Research.
- ICMR-Indian Council of Medical Research.

The study also utilized the database of the available journals, along with the WHO database. The researcher also accesses the government's data and hospital documents on cancer statistics and their reports. The modern turns out to be a cancer hub and the world's largest contributor to cancer mortality rates. The number of cancer-affected people increases every year, while the government has minimal input towards preventive measures against cancer/terminal illness.

Key Words: Terminally ill, Cancer, Mortality Rate, Mental Disharmony, and Emotional Suffering.

Introduction

looking at the current cancer statistics, it is visible that India fought against the cold-blooded killer of 'terminal illness' in the most unsuccessful way. The failures of the health care systems of the country in its terminal diagnosis resulted in making the larger groups of cancer patients face the worst ill experiences one had ever gone through in life. India is the world's largest contributor to cancer mortality with around five lakh deaths per year, mainly due to people's unawareness of the cancer and its symptoms diagnosis policy. However, no proper preventive measures or actions have been taken by the government, though the country is densely populated with terminal illnesses. Moreover, 80% of the cancer population in India lives in rural undeveloped areas with low economic status, who were not able to afford their cancer diagnosis and on the other hand, higher diagnosis fees in India. Thus, undergoing painful terminal illness experiences and living a life of suffering hell without access to any hospitals or clinical diagnosis. The Indian Council of Medical Research, New Delhi, predicted that the number of terminal deaths in the country would increase significantly in the coming years. Moreover, the percentage of cancer patients would likely increase by 20% in India, if the government did not take any immediate quality preventive measures against this cool-blooded killer.

India In the Battle of Terminal Ill Illness: The Present Scenario's

According to the World Health Organization (WHO), cancer or terminal illness is the uncontrolled growth of deadly cells with unstoppable spreads, which destroy every portion of the human body organ one after another. Once the cancerous cells increase and are affected the patient starts losing the functioning of his/her body sites which usually leads to a paralysis condition. These deadly cancer cells expanded through invading the surrounding tissues and spread to other parts of the body by metastasis leading to 8.2 million global deaths a year at present. India has become the world's top contributor to cancer mortality rates with around five lakh terminal deaths per year.[1] Modern India turned out to be a cancer hub with 2.5 million cancer-affected people, which would be expected to increase by 50% in 2025 if the governmental and non-governmental agencies had made no immediate action plan. At present premature death through non-communicable diseases is the leading cause of death in India like cardiovascular ailments, chronic respiratory problems, and diabetes.[2] The cervical and stomach cancer symptoms populations in the Indian state of Mizoram alone are equal to the total numbers of cancer-affected populations in Japan the highest cancer-populated region in the world.[3]

Among the 8.8 million global deaths, India is considered the world's largest contributor to cancer mortality rates.[4] In another finding, around 505,428 to 5, 00,000 cancer patients in India died per year. The main reason for the high cancer mortality rates in India is mainly due to people's unawareness of the treatment procedures for cancer and its symptoms. This is the reason cancer-affected people consult their Oncologists mostly when they are in the terminal stages, which is in the fourth stage of cancer symptoms that are impossible to cure.[5] However, consulting their clinicians in the second stage of cancer diagnosis, patients could have at least 60% for a cure. The interventions of cancer diagnosis in its third stage, the possible rates are reduced to 30% but with the possibility of stage four of cancer within a short time. However, there are no chances for the survivor when it comes to stage four of cancer which gives a maximum life span of 5-7 years. Based on the latest findings of the NICPR report, Breast Cancer and Cervix uterus are the two most common Cancer killers among Indian women. In comparison, Lip/Oral Cavity and Lung Cancer are the two most common killers among Indian men, killing around 2.5 million Indians every year.[6] The last 20 years were the periods where cancer mortality rates have seen rapidly increasing in the country, while the number of cancer incidences has been decreasing in many Western countries. Out of all the cancer mortalities, cervical cancer remains the leading cause of death among Indian men and women followed by Breast cancer mortality.[7]

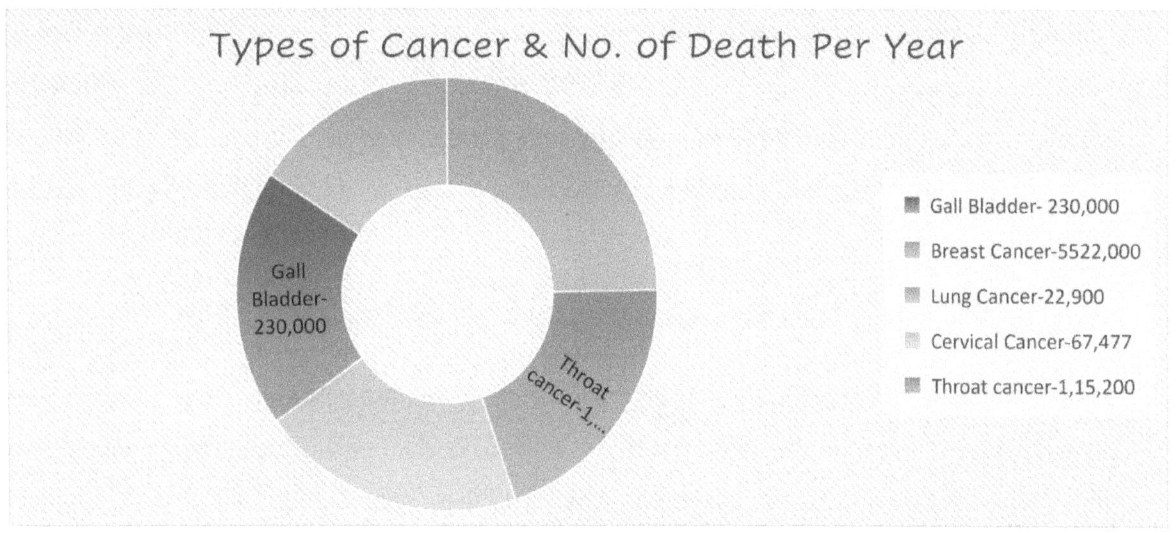

Table I: The Common Types of Cancers and The Numbers of Deaths every year. [4-6]

At present, India is fighting with the cold-blooded killer "Terminal Illness" in the most unsuccessful way. India at present is in critical condition with rapidly increasing rates of one-lakh cancer populations per year and minimal cancer care centers. There are only around 300 regional cancer care centers, which is not enough even to treat one-third of the cancer population in the country. Moreover, India today has only 1000 oncologists, which is a ratio of 1:2000 (one oncologist per two thousand cancer patients). This constituted the underlying reason why modern India turned into a cancer hub. The fight against cancer will continue as the number of affected people rises every year. [8, 9] The following statistic is formed to explain the current cancer status in India:

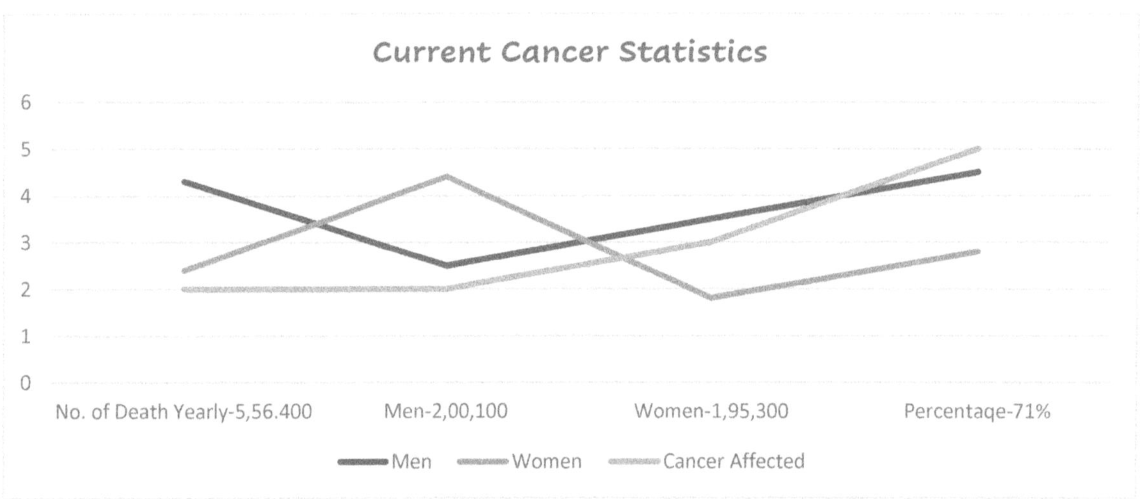

Table 2. Current Cancer Statistic in India. Adapted from NICPR statistical report.

In India, at present one woman dies of Cervical Cancer every 8 minutes. For every newly diagnosed with breast cancer, one out of two women dies in India—moreover, around 2,500 die per day due to cancerous factors like tobacco and bitternut. Smoking, which is the most common practice in India causes 1 in 5 deaths amongst men and 1 in 20 deaths amongst women which constituted around 9,30,000 deaths in 2022. The most productive age period could be highlighted in the ages between 30 and 60 years, which need special consideration, and these age groups need to be targeted the most.[6]

Why is Cancer/Terminal Diagnosis Unsuccessful in India Today?

The main cause of cancer is through internal factors (inherited mutations, hormones, and immune conditions) and external/environmental factors (tobacco, insufficient diet, unhealthy food, organisms, and chemicals with radiation). Among all these components for the causes of cancer and its deadly symptoms, there is a close link between unhealthy food and insufficient diets with cancer disease as observed by many experts.[2] Unhealthy lifestyles with alcohol and smoking are the second most common cancerous factors leading to chronic disease, cardiovascular, lung, kidney, throat, esophagus, and breast cancer. The third common factor for the causes of cancer is visible in excessive consumption of red meats and salted fish leading to heart and breast cancer.[10] At present as per the National Tobacco Control Programmed, tobacco-related cancer illnesses like Heart Attack, Lung Diseases, Stroke, etc. are the common types of cancer in the country. The uses of tobacco cause 100% poor oral health with 90% of mouth cancer, 80% of lung cancer, 50% of all human cancers, 70% of lung diseases, and 60% of heart attacks.[11] The above-mentioned cancerous factors are the most common practices in the Indian Sub-Continent at present, leading to the rapid growth of cancer populations in the country.

Another reason for India being the top cancer populated in the country is mainly due to people's lack of awareness about cancerous components, preventive measures, and the treatment policy. Due to the lack of understanding, most cancer-affected patients detect their cancer symptoms only when the physical pain becomes unbearable, which is in the terminal stages (third or fourth stages) and is impossible to cure. Late detection of cancer symptoms and late cancer diagnosis become the underlying reasons for the 80% of the cancer population failing to cure in India today. However, early detection of the symptoms in its first stage there is an 80% chance of curing. [7]

On the other hand, undergoing cancer diagnosis in the second stage could have a 60% chance for cure, and in the third stage the cure possibility rate is reduced to 30%, but with the possibility of stage four of cancer within a short period. However, in the fourth stage, which is the terminal stage there is no chance to cure, rather to live with the painful symptoms for a maximum life of 5-7 years.[9] The general causes of stomach and cervical cancer symptoms are due to excessive drinking of alcohol, cigarette smoking, and chewing bitternuts. Lung and oral cancer which hugely affect the Indian men and women populations, is mainly due to the excessive use of tobacco, smoking, hookah, and the consumption of locally made alcohol. Another prevailing cancer symptom in India today is nasopharyngeal cancer, which is a malignant cell disease that forms in the tissues of the nasopharynx. Nasopharyngeal cancer (NPC) is the rarest type of cancer around the world, except in Southeast Asia, North Africa, and the Arctic. [10]

The NPC is claimed to be of Chinese origin, which largely affects the Northeast Indian states of Nagaland, Manipur, Mizoram, and to some extent Meghalaya. The state of Nagaland has the highest age-adjusted cancer population with 19.5/100,000, followed by Manipur. Nasopharyngeal cancer is mainly caused by excessive eating of meat, fish, salted fish, use of firewood in the house, and other environmental-related factors like the eating of bitternuts (Kuwa) with or without tobacco products.

Mostly the women populations were mainly affected by nasopharyngeal cancer compared to men. Moreover, within 15-20 years the nasopharyngeal-affected women populations will increase if the uses of tobacco, bitternuts, and the uses of firewood in cooking are not under-controlled. [3,10]

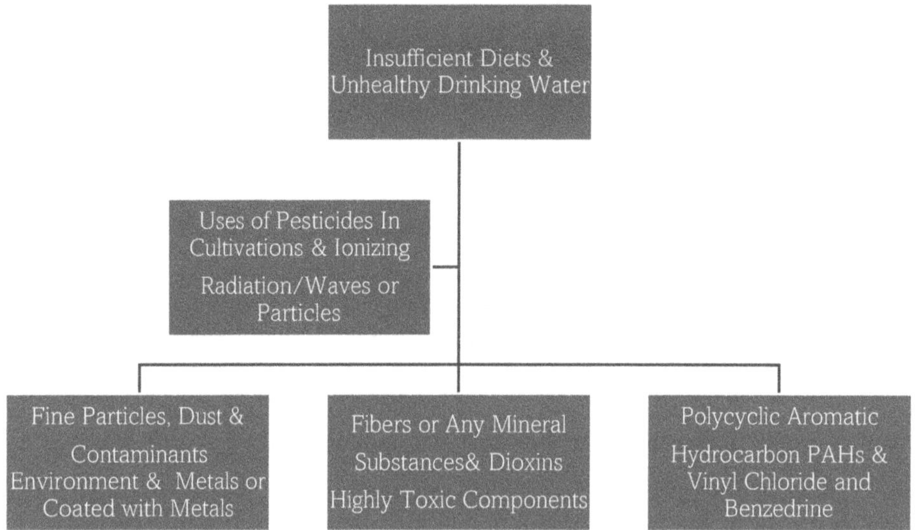

Table 3. The cancerous factors in India as a whole. [12, 13]

Apart from food habits, the population explosion, rapid industrialization, and genetics, which include mutations, and lack of immunity are also responsible for the rapid growth of terminal illness in India as a whole. If proper awareness had not been given mainly to the rural undeveloped areas of the country, there is a possibility of increasing cancer populations to 19% in the next five years. Women have more chances of being affected with cancers than men in India, as per the findings of many. Moreover, the mortality rate of cancers in India is visibly higher among the rural illiterate people group and the maximum number of deaths in India is mainly due to poor prevention strategies and no proper diagnosis as a whole [13] NICRP reported that 122,844 women are diagnosed with cervical cancer every year out of which 67,477 women die from cervical cancer per year. In a population of 432.2 million women in India at present, those women who are aged 15 and above and between 15-40 years are at risk of developing cervical cancer.[14]

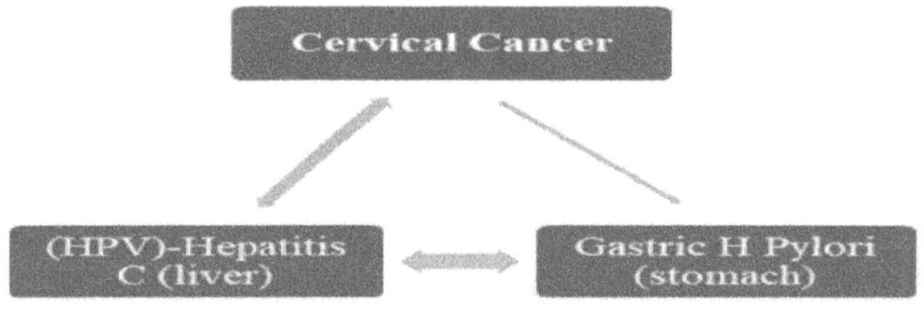

Figure – 4: The two leading Cancer Mortalities in the country

Health scientists, on the other hand, were not able to identify the processes of how risk factors like genetic, hormonal, and environmental factors work together to cause normal cells to become cancerous tumors and cancer symptoms.[10] Thus, cancer has become the leading cause of death in India, with 2.5 million cancer populations, with 1 million cancer patients added every single year. It could be predicted that the number of cancer patients by 2025 will increase by five-fold in India. The rapidly increasing rates of cancer in the country are mainly due to lifestyle risk factors like the use of tobacco, and alcohol, the low fiber in the diet, increasing body weight, minimal physical activities, and the reproductive risk factors regarding age at first pregnancy, and higher numbers of children breastfeeding's. [7,8]

The Proposed Solutions and Preventive Measures

Terminal death is the top cause of Death in India, in the year 2022 India was in the Seventh position among the world's cancer-populated countries. However, due to the rapid increase of cancer populations from 2006-2020, India successfully stood as the highest contributor to world terminal fertility rates, in which the numbers of affected populations are currently visible increasing to 100,000 per year. In recent research findings, only 5-10% of the cancers are from genetics, while the other 90-95% of the cancer-related deadly diseases are from hormonal and environmental factors.[15] This means that 90% of cancer-related diseases can be prevented effectively through proper medical interventions in their early stages and a hygienic lifestyle. Moreover, another 10% of genetic cancerous symptoms can also be prevented through early detection and immediate diagnosis. In short, cancer of any type is curable if detected in its early stages and through proper diagnosis. The following are the qualitative preventive measures to control the rapid growth of cancer in the country: [2, 10]

- Regular medical check-ups, though being in a healthy condition, negligee of regular medical check-ups is visible as the underlying reason for the rapid growth of cancer in the country for the past ten years.
- Educating people with proper awareness strategies, offering effective public health concerns in the schools, and organizing a social meeting to spread cancer awareness. Especially in the rural areas of the country.
- Early detection of the symptom and early medical intervention, because when it comes to the third and fourth stages there is no possibility of a cure.

- Public awareness on active physical activities, exercise for 30 minutes per day, the healthier a person is, the more cells in the body can effectively fight against the invader viruses and bacteria. Regular exercise prevents colon and breast cancer too.

- Minimizing the use of alcohol products, smoking, tobacco, and chewing bitternut products, will minimize the risk of having lung, kidney, throat, esophagus, and breast cancer. It is better to develop a moderate way of consuming 2-3 glasses of alcohol products per day, which will keep oneself away from a heart attack.

- Immunization against hepatitis B virus in infants one to six months old without failure. Neglecting medical treatment for hepatitis B & C can cause chronic illness and liver cancer.

- Developing healthy and safe sexual practices to avoid cancer genesis, unhealthy sexual practices can give birth to cancerous cells.

- Avoiding obesities, such as being grossly fat or overweight, has negative effects on health and makes cells less effective.

- Developing healthy diets, a healthy diet has been scientifically proven to have numerous health benefits and reduce the risk of chronic diseases.

- Reducing occupational and environmental exposures, as excessive exposures to chemicals and their related heavy metals produce ill health. It also affects the future offspring and produces toxicity.

- Avoid excessive consumption of red meats, salt, and long-preserved food. High consumption of red meat, salt, and preserved food leads to diabetes, breast cancer, and obesity.

- Developing the habit of eating fruits regularly, most fruits are less in calories, sodium, and fats. Fruits are essential nutrients like potassium, dietary fibers, vitamin C, and folate (folic acid), which prevent deficiency, and birth defects and help a person to grow with healthy blood pressure.

- For fair skin some avoid exposure to sunlight, wear protective clothing from 10 am to 4 pm, and excessive use of sunscreen creams to be avoided. Failing minimal exposure to sun or UV resulted in many women being diagnosed with skin cancer. On the other hand, excessive exposure to sunlight or UV rays is also dangerous, especially for those having genetic cancerous symptoms.

- Immediate medical intervention on virus and bacterial infections, otherwise the bacteria diseases virus cells usually hide inside the cells and a terminal virus.

The rapid increase of industrialization and urbanization are visible as the two factors leading to the new lifestyle of many Indians, which resulted in increasing the cancer-affected populations in the country. Concerning the current polluted environment, the burden of cancer incidences will gradually increase, as most Indians are not aware of cancerous preventive measures. The only way to prevent Indian men and women from the rapid growth of cancer and its deadly symptoms is to detect the symptoms at the early stages with immediate medical interventions. It is also important to prevent the water and the environment from being polluted by industries and chemicals. However, it could only be possible if the rural populations were educated on cancer awareness and preventive measures. Awareness of overall treatment policies needs multiple efforts from the government and other non-governmental agencies. Moreover, there are over 85,000 synthetic chemicals that are easily available in the market of the country today like cosmetic items flame-retardants, plasticizers in water bottles pesticides in fruits and vegetables, etc. [13,15] On the other hand, 80% of cancer patients in the country were associated with environment factors like exposes to contaminants, unhealthy lifestyle, food, exposed to ionizing radiations, and cleaning of contaminated drainages without any proper preventive measures. Polluting the river to the maximum with several chemicals, and consuming fish from polluted rivers have several cancerous symptoms. Using polluted water from factories or industries for agricultural farming also produces several cancerous components leading to a rapid increase in cancer populations through consuming these agricultural products. Thus, maintaining a healthy environment, healthy lifestyle, healthy food, proper diets, daily exercise, and avoiding tobacco, and smoking. Minimal consumption of alcohol consumption can decrease the rates of cancer-affected populations. The rural areas should avoid using water by dipping hot metal or iron in the blacksmith for washing hands and legs, as it contains cancerous components.

Treatment Policy in Terminal Diagnosis

Cancer patients need immediate access to modern equipment and its therapeutic techniques at the earliest.[15] However, due to the unavailability of the above-mentioned modern cancer treatment equipment in rural Indian care centers, cancer patients fail to quality treatments. Failing the intervention of advanced equipment in terminal diagnosis resulted in ineffective diagnosis in many cases.

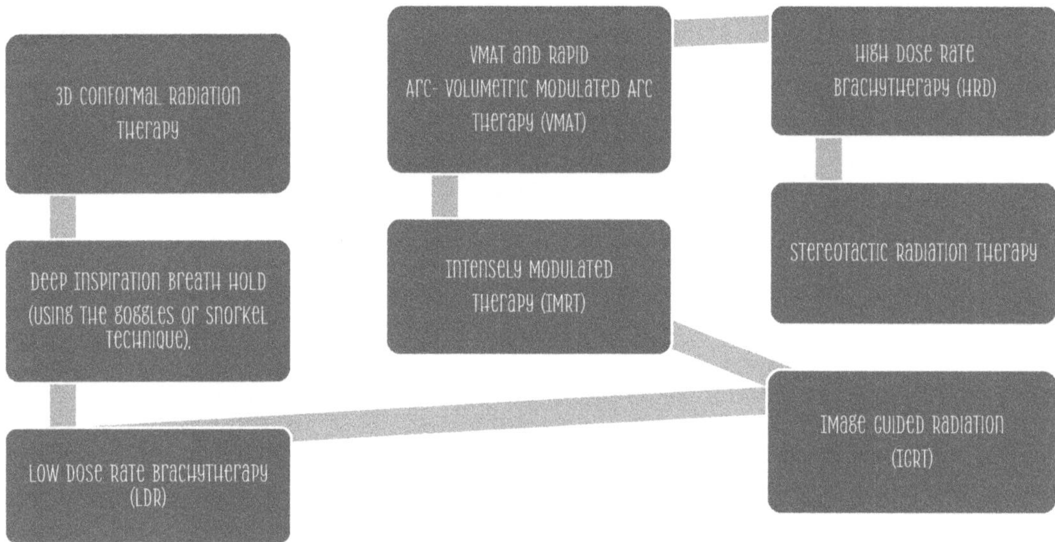

Figure – 5: The WHO Model of Modern Cancer Diagnostic Equipment's. [13]

The quality treatment plan and policy are the core components for successful cancer metastasis diagnosis, which is also visible and ineffective to the minimum. The main emphasis of a cancer diagnosis is to cure the symptoms or to prolong the lives by ensuring quality of life. [13] However, the greatest challenge in Indian cancer diagnosis is the patient's quality of life, which is not visible in the clinical practices of the country. Unnecessary prolonging of the patient's lives to increase the number of days spent in the hospital ward for more bills. Preserving individual value and dignity should be the concern of the clinicians. Patients undergoing treatment against their will/choices need to be rectified immediately in the health care systems of the country.

Early detection and immediate treatment intervention are the two most effective ways of cancer diagnosis to control cancer metastasis and to deliver a total cure. Medical intervention in stages one and two has higher possibility rates of cure and has around 80% cure possibilities as per the finding. Detecting the cancer symptoms and consulting the oncologists in stage three is visible in curtail conditions, having higher impossibility rates as the cancer metastasis accelerates at higher speeds from one body part to another. Having been diagnosed in a stage three patient by a special medical team, it has around a 60% possibility chance of being cured. But does not guarantee complete freedom from cancerous cells, as there is a possibility of being in the terminal stage after three to five months. The reason is that cancer cells have the possibility of hiding under another cell that is hard to detect, resulting in leading one's life to a disability-adjusted life year (DALY).[10] Nevertheless, the detection of the cancer symptoms in the fourth stage has no possible way to cure by any means, which is termed the 'terminal stage' and is 100% impossible to cure in any clinical practice. Thus, resulting in leaving the patient with disability-adjusted life for five to seven years until the inevitable death strikes him/her.

This 5-7 years period of terminal experience is the most crucial moment for every terminal patient, which is also considered the worst moment in a terminal experience with a heartful of emotional suffering and mindful mental disharmony that needs special consideration the most. The acknowledgment of the psycho-emotional symptoms alongside the treatments of physical pain is essential in any terminal diagnosis in clinical practices. At present India turns out to be the worst place to die or a place not to die. The reason is that undergoing cancer/terminal diagnosis's core emphasis is on the physical pain treatment alone, leaving the psycho-emotional pain and suffering untreated. Psychologically distressing symptoms are the byproducts of terminal illness that need special attention. However, the psychosocial distress undergone by all terminal patients is considered the symptoms not to be treated in clinical practices in India. Failing to acknowledge and address the psycho-emotional symptoms resulted in worsening the patient's condition in many ways. [10,13] The concept of total well-being of the whole requires the treatment of patients' mental disharmony and emotional suffering. Psychological well-being can give positive responses to physical pain treatment to the maximum. The psychological self-reflective and life review therapeutic approach in terminal diagnosis can make one aware that he/she is still in the condition of limitless achievements. The person-centered therapeutic assessment will help the patient to recreate his/her life goals and set new goals that could be realistic and achievable. It will also help create beautiful memories with his/her loved ones that deliver quality of life. Above all, it will make dying as normal as birth, which can produce a peaceful and meaningful death.[9] Thus, healing can be delivered as an alternative to cure, even when total cure is impossible in clinical practices. However, sadly, in Indian clinical practices, the clinicians alone are the core medical team without professional clinical psychologists and clinical social workers. [7,9]

Conclusion

The absence of proper medical facilities remains the most challenging and root cause of increasing numbers of cancer/terminal illnesses in the country. Another reason for the rapid increase in rates of cancer and its mortality rates is mainly due to people's unawareness of the causes of cancerous factors, treatment policy, and unhealthy lifestyles. Unhealthy food consumption with no proper preventive measure interventions and absence of diets is the core to unsuccessful diagnosis. Moreover, eliminating the usage of tobacco, cigarettes, and chewing of bitternuts can successfully reduce the rates of oral lip, breast, mouth, cervical, head and neck, and nasopharyngeal (NPC) cancer by at least 40-50%. Another urgent need is to develop social awareness of the causes and treatment policies mainly in the rural areas. Gearing up for health awareness and strengthening the health care team at the community level by addressing the cancer preventive measures will effectively reduce the growing cancer populations.

Hygienic living with healthy food awareness is also an urgent requirement to fight against deadly diseases, with staff conducting seminars in each village at least once a year. Training more oncologists and psycho-oncologists in the country would also be an effective way to fight against the ongoing cancer mortality in the country. The ratio of oncologists and cancer patients in the country is 1:2,000, and the Centre for Cancer Epidemiology in rural areas is at minimal functioning. For the love of humanity, let the terminal diagnosis acknowledge the psycho-emotional suffering and mental disharmony of the patient alongside the physical pain symptoms to deliver the whole person treatment in the clinical practices.

References:

1. World Health Organization. Global Action Against Cancer. http://www.who.int/cancer/media/GlobalActionCancerEnglfull.pdf? Accessed October 25, 2023.

2. Sangita, P Ingole. Aruna, U Kakde. &Priti, B Bonde. A Review on Statistics of Cancer in India. IOSR Journal of Environmental Science, Toxicology and Food Technology. 2016; 10: 107-116. DOI 10.9790/2402-100701107116.

3. Singh Tomcha Th. Cancer Scenario in Northeast India. http://www.epao.net/epsubpageExtractor.asp?src+education.Health_Issue.Scenario_in_Northeast_India. Accessed October 25, 2022.

4. Bhowmick Sourya. 5,00,000 Indians Died of Cancer Last Year. And More Shock Figures. http://www.catchnews.com/india-news/5,00,000-indians-died-of-cancer-last-year-and more-shock-figures. Accessed October 23, 2022.

5. National Institute of Cancer Prevention and Research. India Against Cancer: Statistics. http://cancerinindiadia.org.in/statistics/. Accessed November 12, 2022.

6. Dikshit R, et. al. Cancer mortality in India: A nationally representative survey. The Lancet. https://www.researchgate.net /publication/223989113. Accessed on October 27, 2022.

7. Sreedevi, Aswathy. Javed, Reshma. & Dinesh, Avani. Epidemiology of Cervical Cancer with Special Focus on India. Int J Womens Health. 2015; 7: 405–414. DOI: 10.2147/IJWH.S50001.

8. Deccan Chronicle. Cancer Kills 10 Million In India. Available at: https://www.deccanchronicle.com/lifestyle/health-and-wellbeing/120918/cancer-to-kill-10-mn-in-2018-despite-better-prevention.html. Accessed September 30, 2022.

9. Varghese Cherian. Cancer Prevention and Control in India 50 Years of Cancer Control in India. https://mohfw.gov.in/sites/default/files/Cancer%20Prevention %20And%20Control%20In%20India.pdf. Accessed October 27, 2022.

10. National Tobacco Control Programme. Manipur Has the Highest Tobacco Consumption in India. https://www.ifp.co.in/page/items/8126/8126-manipur-has-the-highest-tobacco-consumption-in-india/. Accessed November 1, 2022.

11. Amal Chandra Kataki, et al. Nasopharyngeal carcinoma in the Northeastern states of India. Chin J Cancer. 2011; 30: 106–113.

12. Bhattacharjee, Abhinandan A. Chakraborty, P. Purkaystha. Prevalence of Head and Neck Cancers in the Northeast-An Institutional Study. Indian Journal of Otolaryngology and Head and Neck Surgery. 2006; 58: 15-19.

13. World Health Organization. WHO List of Priority Medical Devices for Cancer Management: WHO Medical Device Technical Series. http://apps.who.int/iris/bitstream/handle/10665/255262/9789241565462eng.pdf;jsessiond=4A6BE3B164041D129A49E2F006282717?sequence=1. Accessed December 8, 2022.

CHAPTER – TWO

A Good Death: What Constitutes a Meaningful Death

Abstract

End-of-life care is a humanistic approach that aims to deliver a quality of life for patients and families facing life-limiting advanced medical illnesses in clinical practices. It demands a holistic assessment through multidisciplinary team interventions to effectively encounter the patient's psychological sufferings, social isolation, and mental disharmony. The healthcare systems in most of the developed countries were at an advanced stage of delivering 'good death' in the face of painful, and life-threatening medical illness. However, end-of-life care is still an unheard area of care in most parts of the Indian subcontinent. The goal is not to shorten or prolong the patient's life but to focus on alleviating pain and improving quality of life. Yet, 80% of the terminally ill patients in India failed to receive end-of-life care, failing to deliver the quality of life. Effective implementation of plans and policies, maximum availability of essential medications, and public awareness are the current challenges in Indian palliative end-of-life care.

Key Words: End-of-Life Care, Symptoms, Dying Patient, Ethical Principles, and Quality of Life

Introduction

Death in the modern era has evolved from home to hospital and other nursing care centers with the advance of medical technologies. End-of-life care is a worldwide phenomenon that helps in improving the patient's quality of life and well-being of the whole for those with advanced medical illnesses like HIV and cancer. The primary aim of end-of-life care is to acknowledge the several dimensions of a patient's need, such as physical pain and symptom control, safeguarding the ethical norms regarding death and dying, and the legal principles in critical care. However, India is still considering a place not to pass by many. Dying with dignity and good death are the two unheard topics of discussion in most Indian healthcare systems. Palliative end-of-life care in India at present is visible as the most neglected area of care, and 80% of the total population has not accessed it so far.

The present discussion focused on "good death," "successful dying" or "meaningful dying." Is successful dying an extension of successful aging? Research on successful aging has grown considerably in recent years, though little agreement as to what specifically constitutes a good death or successful dying despite many reviews examining the concept of a good death from sociological and philosophical viewpoints. The current research examining the quality of death and dying, which is defined as "the degree to which a person's preferences for dying and the moment of death agree with observations of how the person died, as reported by others." The goal is to examine the definitions of a good death from the perspectives of patients, their family members, and healthcare providers (HCPs).

Defining End-Of-Life Care

The recent advances in medical technology, diagnostics, and other related antibiotic therapies created bioethical dilemmas confronting clinicians in critical care units. Due to the new advancements in modern medicine, the process of dying has become more prolonged, and an increasing number of people require long-term care for chronic conditions. On the other hand, clinicians are less trained in providing holistic assessment while encountering the psycho-emotional sufferings, social isolation, and spiritual disharmony experienced by dying patients. End-of-life care is an interdisciplinary medical field focusing on preventing and relieving psycho-emotional suffering and mental conflict for patients/families dealing with advanced medical illnesses. It is a supportive care approach aiming to deliver a quality of life and work in the interest of the patient and family.[1] Effective end-of-life care requires both hospice and palliative care that helps those with life-threatening incurable medical illnesses to live as well as possible until the inevitable death strikes. Within the healthcare community and, more specifically, in hospice and palliative care, there has been some discussion of the concept of a good death. The concept arose from the hospice movement and has been described as a multifaceted and individualized experience. According to an Institute of Medicine, a good death is "free from avoidable distress and suffering for patient, family, and caregivers, in general accord with the patient's and family's wishes, and reasonably consistent with clinical, cultural, and ethical standards." [2]

Modern hospice care is an interdisciplinary, integrated approach that aims at caring for rather than curing those facing the end of life. Hospice care focuses on treating the person and symptoms of the disease rather than the disease itself. The hospice involves a team-oriented approach to expert medical care, pain management, and psychological and spiritual support personalized to the patient's needs and wishes. The core concept of hospice care accepts death as the final stage of human life and affirms it neither hastens nor postpones death. Hospice care is also family-centered and includes the patient and the family in decision-making at any level. [2,3] Palliative care is not for patients near the end of life alone but in acute and long-term settings. The World Health Organization (WHO) states that palliative care is an approach that improves the quality of life of the patients and their families facing the problems associated with life-threatening illnesses. Early identification and impeccable assessment of pain and non-pain symptoms (psychological, Social, and spiritual) can effectively prevent and relieve the patient from their ill experiences. [4] Unlike hospice, palliative care can be provided at any stage of an illness and extended to the family bereavement period.

Palliative end-of-life Care in India

End-of-life care in India originated in Shanti Avedna Sadan in Mumbai, founded in 1986 by Lucito D'Souza. The second phase of its development was in Kerala, with the formation of the Pain and Palliative Care Society in 1993 in Calicut and the Indian Institute of Palliative Care in 1994. The first free Palliative Care service in North India was in 1997 in Delhi, while the Guwahati Pain and Palliative Care Society became the first in the North-East Indian region. The formation of Pallium India in 2003 was another milestone for the establishment of palliative care centers in another eleven states of the country through its charitable organization. In 2010 the Medical Council of India accepted palliative end-of-life care medicines as an integrated course in medical sciences. However, the Ministry of Health in 2012 advocated that the National Program for Palliative Care was merely theoretical propaganda with minimal implementation. The underlying reason could be negligence and insufficient funds from the government with minimal awareness of educating the general population. [5,6]

At present, palliative end-of-life care is visible functioning in 16 states intending to relieve physical pain symptoms alone. The state of Kerala alone has 230 clinics located in 12 districts, which cater to only 3% of the total population.[7] In 2008 the Indian public health system, in collaboration with WHO and other non-governmental organizations, made some efforts to develop manual guidelines for palliative care services at the hospital and community levels. It was also to improve the existing guidelines on palliative care and quality pain management in the country. The collaboration resulted in the formation of the National Programme for Palliative Care (NPPC) under the National Health Mission (NHM) in 2012. The program operates under the National Programme for Prevention and Control of Cancer, CVD, Diabetes, and Stroke (NPCDCS), with a provision for establishing palliative end-of-life care services in every district hospital in the country. It was to set up palliative end-of-life care centers, distributed in a 60:40 proportion between the Centre and state, while 90:10 in the North-Eastern parts of the country.[8] As per the 2017 report, West Bengal, Kerala, and Assam were visible setting up the operationalizing palliative care units in selected district hospitals. The technical support and training of the health care professionals are the two contributing factors for the advocacy and raising awareness of palliative end-of-life care in the country. Thus, three types of palliative end-of-life care are visible and available in the country: Home-Based Care, Outpatient Services, and Hospice Care Services. But all are with minimal functioning. Home-based care is one of the effective ways patients in rural areas can access palliative end-of-life care. In the WHO report, India in 2020 had around 60 million people above 65 years, increasing to 227 million by 2050, constituting 20% of the total population. However, lack of palliative care facilities, poor quality of death index, and lack of medical infrastructure, India has become a place not to die for many.[9]

The Legal Position of End-of-Life Care in India

Since its infancy, palliative end-of-life care was a neglected area of care in the country; there were no sound legal principles around death and dying until the Aruna Shambaugh case (a nurse who was gang raped and lived in a vegetative state for 42 years in Mumbai). It would be true to say that it was in 2009 that the Supreme Court passed the bill for the first time allowing passive euthanasia on the 42-year-old vegetative patient Aruna Shambaugh however, the government accepted passive euthanasia, but only in a few exceptional cases. It also stated that euthanasia was never a law in this country. With strict instructions, the Supreme Court on March 2011 and July 16, 2014, issued a public notice on legalizing passive euthanasia that allows the patient and the family to withdraw the ongoing medical treatment only to those who are in a vegetative state and need to be in the rarest case in its clinical practices. [10,6]

Another legal challenge in end-of-life care lies in the issue of death and dying. Based on the Transplantation of the Human Organs Act of 1994, the end of the patient is when they permanently lose the evidence of life and living, regarding the death of the brain stem or in the case of cardio-pulmonary, which is when the blood circulation and the breathing stop functioning in the dying individual. Section 46 of the Indian Panel Code, death of a person, is when the normal organs in the human body stop working, but the code also holds onto its situational ethics on end. The brain stem here mainly refers to the part of the human brain responsible for breathing. However, the Indian Legislation Section 2 (b) of the Birth and Death Registration Act of 1969 holds that the death of the brain stem alone is not a good criterion to declare a person as deceased. The Act acknowledges the process of ventilation breathing as life under living and cannot be pronounced dead. [11,12] Sometimes, in the Intensive Care Unit, patients experience the death of the brain stem but still breathe with the help of ventilation, which could be living from the heart. The best example is in the Aruna Shamburg case, a girl who survived and breathed for 42 years even after the death of her brain stem.

Based on the 196th report of The Law Commission of India in 2006, a patient declaring their "Advance Will" was strictly prohibited mainly to avoid misusing it for personal gain. On the other hand, the joint statement of The Indian Society of Critical Care Medicine (ISCCM) and the Indian Association of Palliative Care (IAPC) stated that at present, there are no proper guidelines for the provision of the moral and ethical dilemmas with regards to end-of-life care, especially in the policy connected to euthanasia. However, the Law Commission of India, in their 241st report of 2012, permitted the practices of euthanasia, which would be mainly based on humanitarian grounds and the law also agrees to protect those medical practitioners who genuinely act for the best interest of the dying patient and the family. The definition of euthanasia as per the Law Commission of India is mercy killing through the help of lethal drugs used in clinical practices on the sincere request of the patient, in which the family is not permissible to make any decision in connection to euthanasia on the patient's behalf. However, the definition of euthanasia given by the Forgoing of Life Support Treatments (FLSTs) proposes a process of 'letting die of the patient' without the intervention of any other factors, and refusal of the ongoing medical treatment does not mean attempting suicide either. Even though in the last phase of the patients in end-of-life commonly experience loss of sense and cannot decide on their own, the right to act on the patient's behalf is given to none. [13,14]

The Ethical Principles/Issues in End-Of-Life Care

Justice in palliative end-of-life care is the underlying concern for the well-being of the whole and enhances the patient's quality of life. It is an appropriate assessment of the patient to maximize the patient's welfare through an integrated approach and avoid unproductive evaluations in clinical practices. In end-of-life care, the responsibility of the clinicians is not to fulfill every wish of the patients, but instead to maintain the medical ethics, policy, and professional treatment standard in any given situation. On the other hand, the law also upholds that physicians in end-of-life care settings are strictly advised not to go against the patient's will/choices regarding the refusal of the ongoing medical treatment even if it causes the patient's death. Apart from providing detailed medical treatment information to the patient, the clinicians are bound to involve the patient in any treatment-related decision-making part.[15] The law demands that physicians always act in the patient's best interest without any obligation and deliver a good death by giving the patient and the family to prepare well for the inevitable end. Medical ethics is a set of rules that govern the activities of medical professionals and perform their tasks according to the medical standard through its moral principles. The patient has a full right to know the details of their diagnosis and either accept the treatment or refuse it.[14]

Medical ethical principles are not a law but a guiding factor that has the utmost importance in caring for those with medically advanced illnesses like HIV and cancer. The Indian Palliative End-of-Life Care laid its ethical foundation on patient autonomy, beneficence, non-malfeasance, social justice, and appropriate treatment. The patient's autonomy constitutes an important domain in palliative end-of-life care. It is self-right and self-respect to be independent, mainly regarding decision-making on treatment policy. The patient's autonomy requires their presence as an active member of the medical management team and decision-making. Autonomy gives the patient a sense of authority over their illness, risks versus benefits, and the core deciding factor to outweigh the burdensome issues. It is also important for the physicians working in end-of-life care to act for the patient's welfare and what benefits the dying patient and family the most by knowing all the truthful information about the medical treatment policy or the patient's condition. Since palliative end-of-life care aims not to shorten nor prolong patient life but to deliver the quality of life and well-being of the whole through any possible means, physicians should possess adequate knowledge of pain and symptom management. However, relieving the pain and distress of the patient through mercy killing or by any means is not an option; the ethical principle, on the other hand, allows the use of opioids to do away with the pain and distressful symptoms. [11]

Non-malfeasance is the state of doing no harmful activities while attending to the needs of the palliative end-of-life care patient. It avoids ineffective medical treatment with no possible benefits that would possibly increase the risk factors in the terminal diagnosis. The prime focus in end-of-life care is to make dying more meaningful rather than a fearful or dreadful inpatient experience. The process of dying in individual experience should be when they find meaning in suffering and time all the various needs of the dying individual addressed and taken care of through any possible means. It is also important for the health care providers to earn the trust of their patients, which would help in having quality communication where the patient can share their thoughts and wishes without hesitation. [4,12] Even in the last phase of terminal illness diagnosis, where patients normally lose their sense and ability to decide on their own, clinicians should respect and value. The principle compelled the physicians not to continue aggressive life-prolonging or withdrawal of the ongoing treatment without the patient's concern. Fair treatment gives the right to claim what they are legitimately entitled to, which is the core emphasis of the ethical principle in end-of-life care. [12]

A Good Death: What Constitutes a Meaningful Death?

End-of-life care for the quality of life and death is still an unheard topic in most Indian clinical settings. Developed countries like the UK, USA, Canada, Australia, etc., are at the advanced stage aiming to deliver "good death" in the face of painful terminal experiences. A meaningful death is free from death anxiety, distress, and suffering consistent with cultural and ethical norms. Death anxiety is the degree of anxiety regarding the anticipation of death, which is persistent and interferes with everyday life functioning, also commonly understood as the fear of death or the fear of the dying process. The signs and symptoms can be visible in solicitude, dread, extreme timidness, and distress that cause disorder, which requires a maximum amount of care and emotional support. A good death is a meaningful dying process that occurs when the patient is physically, psychologically, spiritually, and emotionally supported by their family, caregivers, and friends. [7,11] In one research finding successful dying or good death has three main preferences for the dying process: Avoiding prolonged dying process (94% of reports), pain-free status (81%), and Spiritual/Emotional well-being (64%). The following are the elements of a good death in clinical practices: [10,14]

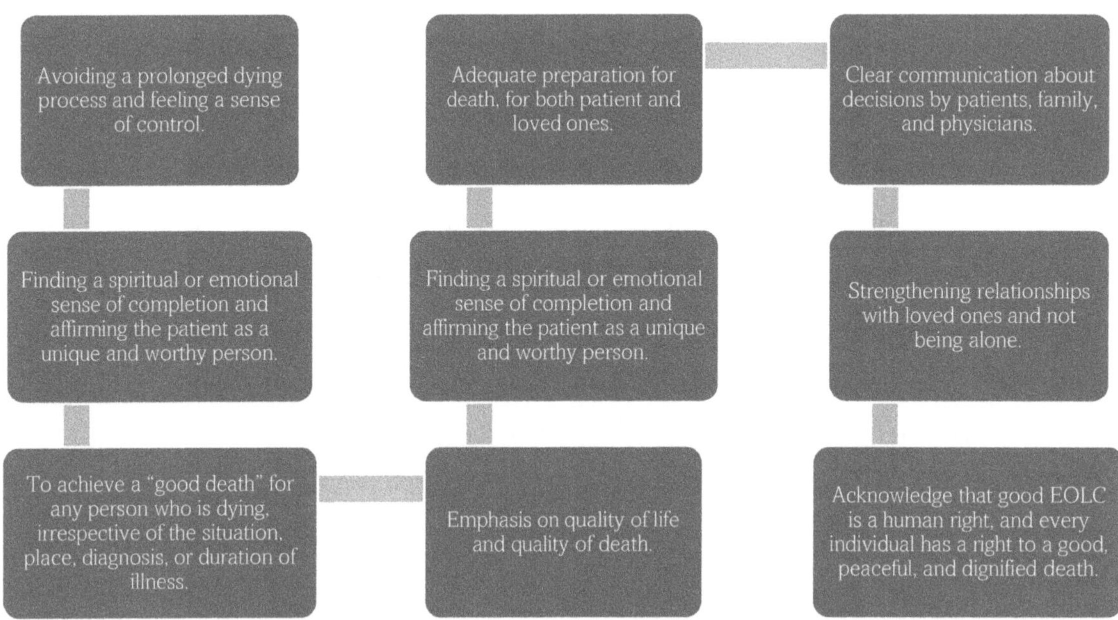

<u>Figure – I: Adequate Pain and Symptom Management.</u>

However, many religions and legal systems do not encourage knowing when death is coming and being prepared for another element of a good death. Respecting the wishes of dying patients and allowing them to choose death could also be another practical element in delivering a good end. Such a provision does not exist in India as it is considered taboo, resulting in India being a place not to die by many. However, an appeal had been submitted to the Supreme Court on allowing advance directive care in the Indian clinical setting. The following are the infrastructures required for effective end-of-life care in clinical practices: [15]

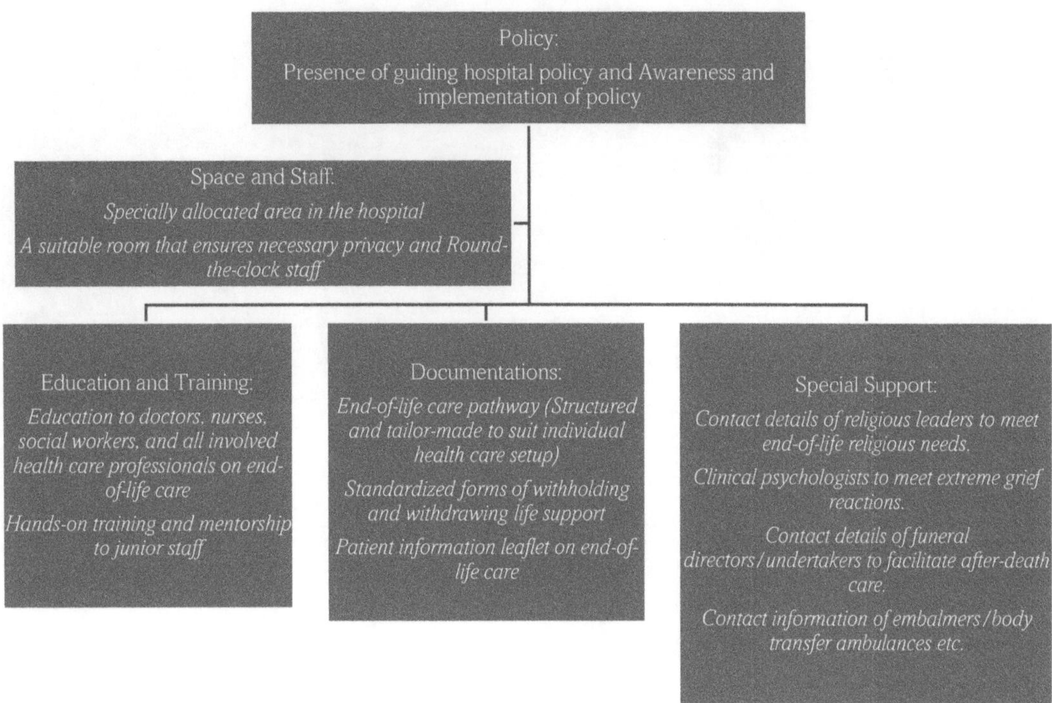

<u>Figure – 2: Quality Infrastructure Plan for End-of-Life Care</u>

Looking at the current situation, most terminally ill patients in India experience a disadvantage in dying. The reason is the absence of 'good death' principles and infrastructural requirements in Indian palliative end-of-life care. The disadvantage of dying refers to the group of people whose physical, social, and spiritual care is at risk of being undermined or neglected because of societal attitude, ignorance, or discrimination at their end of life. Most commonly, people with HIV/AIDS, learning disabilities, older people, most commonly cancer patients from poverty, and dementia. Even the LGBTQ community is also at greater risk. Thus, modern India fails to deliver holistic assessment in its clinical practices.

The Current Challenges and Discussion

The misconception about palliative care confining mainly to end-of-life care is the most significant challenge in India. This misconception is common even among oncologists and physicians, resulting in failing to refer needed patients to palliative care. Palliative care aims to provide the best possible quality of life at every stage of treatment in clinical practices. Several positive outcomes have been visible to those with access to palliative care at the early stages. Such misconceptions or the lack of awareness even among medical practitioners fail to acknowledge the maximum number of patients and families with no access to seek relief during their diagnosis period.[10]

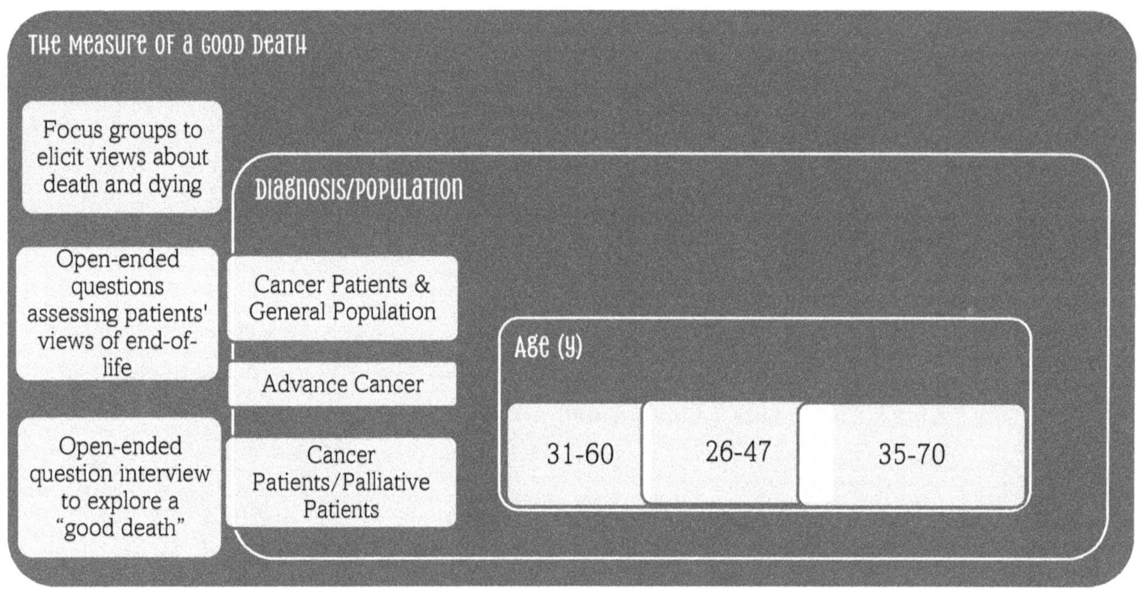

Figure – 3: Factors Measuring a Good Death in End-of-Life Care

Palliative end-of-life care is the most neglected area of care in Indian medical care. Only 1%-2% of the total population in India has access to end-of-life care or total pain symptom management. Even most Indian medical students also failed to access the curriculum on pain management. The use of opioids for managing severe pain in terminal ill-treatment and major trauma needs special consideration among medical students and other clinicians. The need of the hour is to effectively implement the end-of-life care policy and plan, availability of essential medicines and medical facilities, public education, and awareness. The proper implementation of end-of-life care will avoid unnecessary medical expenses, like undergoing chemotherapy at the final stage of terminal illness diagnosis. The unavailability of essential drugs for pain management in palliative end-of-life care in some parts of the Indian sub-continent needs special consideration. [4,6]

In health and well-being, India had several issues to deal with, mainly in pain and non-pain symptom management. Modern India turns out to be a cancer hub with 2.5 million cancer-affected people, which is likely to increase by 50% in 2020 if the governmental and non-governmental agencies have no immediate action plan. Once the killer cells grow and affect the patient's start losing their body sites, it usually leads to a paralyzing condition, requiring a multidisciplinary team for the treatment procedures.[14] On the other hand, dying with dignity or a peaceful death in the Indian health care system is an alien term, mainly due to the absence of pain and symptom management in its medical syllabus for undergraduate and postgraduate medical students. The minimum availability of palliative end-of-life care centers and the higher rates of medical treatment fees are also the underlying reasons for many terminally ill patients not receiving end-of-life care. The need is to integrate psychosocial aspects of palliative end-of-life care as a primary health education syllabus for undergraduate medical professionals in the country.

Conclusion

The country's health care system should incorporate psychological non-pain symptom management as a compulsory syllabus for undergraduate medical practitioners. Integration of societal involvement and addressing the psycho-spirituality needs in palliative end-of-life care is also an important domain and the immediate needs of the dying patient for the quality of life, well-being of the whole, peace, and dying with dignity. The negligence of the holistic needs of the dying patients in end-of-life care in the medical-related curriculums needs an immediate revitalization to deliver the whole person treatment and quality of life.

The inclusion of the syllabus like effective clinical management in terminal diagnosis, peaceful death, dying with dignity, dealing with several mental disharmonies, and psychological issues in the undergraduate and post-graduation medical curriculum are also significant challenges. Exceptional attention should be on the various dimensions of the patient's needs while maintaining the country's ethical principles and legal norms and uplifting the urgent necessity of palliative end-of-life care in India today.

Reference

1. Yeolekar ME, Mehta S, Yeolekar A. End of Life Care: Issues and Challenges. Journal of Postgraduate Medicine. 2008; 54 (3): 173-175. DOI: 10.4103/0022-3859.41795.

2. Field MJ, Cassel CK, editors. Approaching Death: Improving Care at the End of Life. Washington, DC: National Academy Press; 1997.

3. NCPPC-National Clinical Programme for Palliative Care. Palliative Care Needs Assessment Guidance. Retrieved from the web January 2022. www.hse.ie/eng/service/publications/ clinical-strategy-and-programes/palliative-care-needs-assessment-guidance.pdf.

4. American Cancer Society. What is Hospice Care? https://www.cancer.org/treatment/end-of-life-care/hospice-care/what-is-hospice-care.html. Retrieved from the web January 2023.

5. World Health Organization. WHO Definition of Palliative Care. who. in/cancer/palliative/definition/en. Accessed from the web on February 11, 2023.

6. Rajagopal M R. WHO Collaborating Centre for Training and Policy on Access to Pain Relief, Pallium, Thiruvananthapuram, Kerala, India. Indian Journal of Palliative Care. 2016; 22 (3): 239-243. DOI: 10.4103/0973-1075.185025.

7. Khosla D Patel, D Firuza, Sharma C Suresh. Palliative Care in India: Current Progress and Future Needs. Indian Journal of Palliative Care. 2012; 18 (3): 149-154. DOI: 10.4103/0973-1075.105683.

8. Ministry of Health and Family Welfare, PIB Delhi. Palliative Care Units for Cancer Patients. https://pib.gov.in/PressReleaseIframePage.aspx?PRID=1498830/2017. Accessed February 2, 2020. Retrieved from the web January 2023.

9. Myatra Nainan Sheila et al. End-of-life care policy: An integrated care plan for the dying A Joint Position Statement of the Indian Society of Critical Care Medicine (ISCCM) and the Indian Association of Palliative Care (IAPC). Indian J Crit Care Med. 2014; 18(9): 615–635. Doi: 10.4103/0972-5229.140155.

10. Mani RK. Constitutional and Legal Protection for Life Support Limitation in India. Indian J Palliat Care. 2015 Sep-Dec; 21(3): 258–261. Doi: 10.4103/0973-1075.164903.

11. The Law Commission of India. The 196th Report on Medical Treatment to Terminally Ill Patients (Protection of Patients and Medical Practitioners). http://lawcommissionofindia.nic.in/reports/rep196.pdf. Accessed on 22 November 2023.

12. APCA-African Palliative Care Association. A Handbook of Palliative Care in Africa, 2010. Eds. Julia Dowling et al. http://aidsfree.usaid.gov.pdf. Accessed on 27th December 2022.

13. Center for Bioethics, University of Minnesota. End-of-Life Care: An Ethical Overview, 2005. www.ahc.umn.edu/img/assets/26104/End_of_Life.pdf. Accessed on 27th January 2022.

14. Puchalski C M. Spirituality and End-of-Life Care: A Time for Listening and Caring. Journal of Palliative Care Medicine. 2002; 5 (2), 289-294. DOI: 10.1089/109662102753641287.

15. Chochinov, Max Harvey. Dying, Dignity, and New Horizons in Palliative End-of-Life Care. CA A Cancer Journal for Clinicians. 2006; 56 (2): 84-103..

16. Meier Emily A, Gallegos Jarred V, Thomas Lori P. Montross, et al. Defining a Good Death (Successful Dying): Literature Review and a Call for Research and Public Dialogue. American Journal of Geriatric Psychiatry. 2016; 24 (4): 261-271. DOI: 10.1016/j.jagp.2016.01.135

CHAPTER – THREE

Holistic Assessment in Palliative End-Of-Life Care

Abstract

The present increasing numbers of terminal illnesses and chronic diseases gave rise to the importance of holistic assessment in Indian clinical settings. In the era of advanced modern medicine and its components, people still die in distress as their mental disharmony and psychological suffering are not considered symptoms to be treated. Dying should be as normal as birth, but not in Indian clinical settings. India turned out to be a country not to die as people died in vulnerable conditions. The absence of holistic treatment in Indian palliative end-of-life care resulted in clinicians treating the physical pain symptom alone, leaving the psychosocial-spiritual symptoms untreated. The holistic assessment is a 'total care' or a 'whole person treatment,' which includes the treatment of physical pain, psychological suffering, mental disharmony, social values, and spiritual symptoms in palliative end-of-life care. The holistic assessment is based on the unique principle that every human has different worldviews, having values, opinions, beliefs, and perspectives that need to be acknowledged and given special treatment until the inevitable death attack. Thus, the holistic assessment not only enhances the quality of life but also serves as a platform for terminally ill patients can experience genuine choice and quality decision-making in the face of inevitable death.

Key Words: Assessment, Total Care, Symptoms, Depression, Stress, and Anxiety

Introduction

Looking at the current conditions of palliative end-of-life care in India, the primary care concern is the physical pain symptom alone. The whole person's treatment is an unheard therapy as the psychological suffering, mental disharmony, spiritual needs, and social issues, which purely control the total well-being of a terminal patient were not acknowledged as symptoms to be treated. The primary objective of palliative end-of-life care as described by the World Health Organization (WHO) is not to prolong life, but rather to deliver a quality of life and a good death. However, in Indian clinical practices, the terminal diagnosis is confined to the physical pain symptom alone, failing to produce a quality of life and a good death in the patient terminal experience. The exclusion of the terminal patient's psycho-emotional and socio-spiritual suffering in the terminal diagnosis will sometimes result in worsening the physical health condition of the patient. The terminal experience is the worst experience one must go through, it is occupied with several ill feelings like isolation, depression, meaninglessness, burdensome, and social stigma, which deliver mental disharmony. [1,2] It requires the interventions of multiple assessments such as physical, psychological, spiritual, and social assessments to deliver the quality of life in clinical practices. The whole person's treatment provides symptom relief and alleviates suffering by delivering total care and making death as normal as birth.

Assessment in Palliative End-of-Life Care: Meaning and Concept

Assessment in the end-of-life is a process of a holistic approach to care, which provides an opportunity for those with life-limiting terminal illness and their families to explore and identify the best approach to care to meet their needs [1]. It is a process of discovering the limitless possibilities that could be achieved through suffering with terminal experience and in the face of inevitable death. It is an ongoing person-centered care by acknowledges the total pain in terminal diagnosis including the physical pain, the psychological suffering, spiritual need, and the issue of socio-cultural stigma in the patient terminal experience until the inevitable death attack. In contradiction to the confusion on who to access, when, where, and what, the assessment should be given to every patient suffering from a life-limiting terminal illness irrespective of their age or setting. The primary focus of the holistic assessment is to discover what the patient perceives to be his/her problems, concerns, and needs, and find out how the patient could be prioritized in his/her life-limiting terminal experience. [2,3]

Holistic assessment can be assessed in any physical setting, either at home or in the clinical setting. However, it is important to ensure the comfort and privacy of the patient and its main aim is to minimize or relieve the patient from physical pain and psycho-emotional suffering to deliver quality of life. Palliative end-of-life care is holistic care focusing on trans-cultural, comprehensive, and patient-centered therapy depending on the needs and concerns of the patient and family. [2] In assessing a life-limited terminally ill patient, it is important to have proper Advance Care Planning (ACP) that gives the freedom for the patient to discuss the most appropriate approach of care as per the needs and concerns of the patient and family. The discussion on ACP should fulfill the individual's concerns, patient values, or personal goals, and understanding about patient illness and prognosis. [4,5] In providing quality and meaningful assessment in end-of-life care, it must be regularly and should be delivered in painful situations when the symptoms are often uncontrolled. However, at some point due to the lack of proper patient caring knowledge and the absence of proper training in end-of-life care among clinicians, the healthcare professionals are unwilling to diagnose terminally ill patients who are nearing death and remain helpless. [6]

Important Domain in Palliative End-of-Life Care

There is no easy way to deliver a quality of life to those experiencing the most unwanted experience one must go through in his/her life. Moreover, caring for the distressing physical pain, discomfort, and psychological symptoms like emotional suffering and mental disharmony in the clinical settings, requires maximum amounts of effort and attention attained by the multidisciplinary teams, which is not visible in the context of Indian palliative end-of-life care at present. No doubt that in terminal illness or chronic diseases, physical pain is one of the most common symptoms due to the weak body being unable to restore the amount of energy to bear it. Pain becomes the most prominent risk factor for depression, change in behavior, and suicide for those with chronic or terminal illness, which need special consideration for quality of life. Sadly, looking at the current Indian clinical setting, the primary aim is on physical pain symptoms alone and leaving the psycho-spiritual need for healing. However, the WHO on palliative end-of-life care stated that to improve quality of life the illness and all the problems associated with the illness need equal treatment. Psychological assessment can effectively deal with depression, stress disorder, anxiety, emotional disorder, and mental disharmony for both the patient and the family. Ensuring the psychological well-being of the patient will lead to effective physical pain treatment and deliver quality of life. Moreover, most people coping with cancer or life-limiting terminal illness usually experience severe psychological distress, which is a unique discomforting emotional state to a specific stressor or demand harming the individual permanently or temporarily. [7,8,9]

For those facing or coming near the end of life, psychological distress is mostly manifested in the form of depression, anxiety, and adjustment disorder. In the journey of terminal illness, patients usually experience being alone in the continuum which results in experiencing fear, sadness, and grief leading to worsening their ill condition. [8]

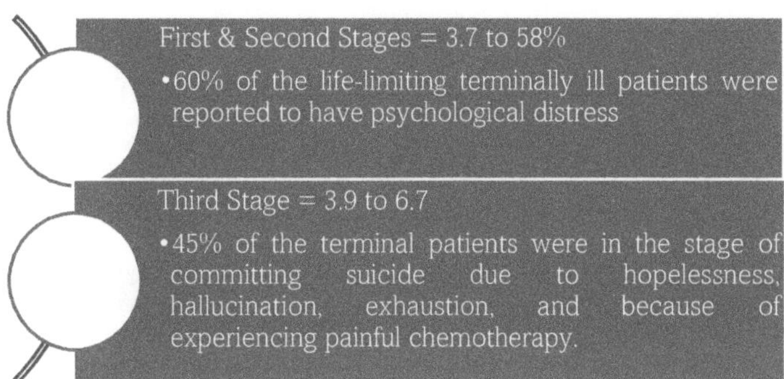

More than 60% of the life-limiting terminally ill patients were reported having psychological distress because of their illness and 50% of the patients consulted their psychiatrist, out of which 45% of the terminal patients were in the stage of committing suicide due to hopelessness, hallucination, exhaustion, and because of experiencing painful chemotherapy. [7] Unlike any other symptoms, depression is multifaceted and multidimensional in its functioning. In the Western world, depression-measuring instruments like CES-D, HADS, and BD-II, are developed mainly to stress out the patient's nature of depression and positively influence the cognitive, somatic, and behavioral domains of one's life in the face of terminal and chronic illness. [8] Looking at the present condition of palliative end-of-life care in India, symptoms like depression and other psychologically related symptoms are considered symptoms not to be treated in its clinical practices. Depression can be successfully taken care of in a higher proportion only through the elimination of the distressing symptoms, with emotional support and counseling, which could explore fear and its components more appropriately. [9] Therefore, psychological assessment in end-of-life care is always an important domain of care to deal with the neuro-vegetative symptoms of depression and the process of treatment. It not only improves the patient's mental and emotional moods but also enhances their coping strategy which promotes their conformity with treatments.

Another important domain of holistic care is the spiritual needs of the dying patients, as end-of-life care is a holistic approach of care that does not limit its approaches to the physical, cultural, psychological, and economic needs, but also to the spiritual needs of the dying individual. Mostly, terminally ill patients acknowledge a greater spiritual perspective and orientation than those with healthy and non-terminally ill hospitalized patients. It is not necessarily important to link spirituality always with religious beliefs and sacred practices, like the current common concept of spirituality in Indian society and cultures, which relates and binds spirituality only within the religious beliefs' realm. Recently, the WHO has declared spirituality as an important dimension for quality of life in end-of-life care, and a tenet of palliative care. In broader terms, spirituality is a mechanism that operates one's thoughts and feelings regarding one's well-being and purpose, based merely on the individual's philosophies of life, rather than the established faith and religion. Thus, spirituality in palliative end-of-life care is more about finding meaning, hope, comfort, and inner peace in one's life to deliver a quality of life. The primary concern is to deliver the patient's sense of purpose in life in any given environment. [11, 4, 12]

Many of the existing documents and literature have recognized and described spirituality as the dominant factor in contributing to a patient's positive health. It is also an effective coping mechanism against depression, suicidal feelings, pain, and suffering for terminally ill patients, especially those nearing death. The spiritual psychotherapeutic is a subjective experience that exists both within and outside the traditional religious systems. [13] The following are the important principles that need to be assessed in delivering spiritual psychotherapeutics for those who are facing their end-of-life:[14,15]

a) Principles of spiritual assessment include examining the importance of organized religion in a person's life, his/her private religious or spiritual practices, along those non-traditional spiritual practices. It is also important to acknowledge the intrinsic or extrinsic orientation of a patient's spirituality and its practices.

b) Investigation of individual spiritual identity refers to one sense of divine worth and its potentiality, as it is particularly important for the palliative care populations in the clinical setting.

c) The spirituality psychotherapeutic involves the examination of the patient's inner resources on how the spiritual/religious beliefs, attitudes, and practices influence one's reaction to and with death and dying.

d) The importance of examining the patient spiritual problem-solving style such as Self-Directing, Deferring, and Collaborative, to know whether the patient is fully independent and entirely rely to God for remedy and healing or the patient being in partnership with God to arrive at solution.

e) It is important to acknowledge the functions of spiritual measurement scale and sub-scales, such as the Functional Assessment of Chronic Illness Therapy-Spiritual Well-Being Scale, along with the Meaning and Faith Sub-Scale. These spiritual measurement scales and sub-scales address the overarching dimension of spirituality, the inner serenity, and peace within oneself. It also measures the extent to which individuals find comfort and strength in their beliefs.

f) There are three important aspects of patient needs: Situational, Moral/Biographical, and Religiosity. The situational need relates to finding purpose, hope, and meaning. Reconciliation in relationships, prayer, moral, social analysis, divine forgiveness, closure, support, religious rites/sacraments, visits by clergy, meditating on religious literature, and discussion about God, eternal life, and purpose, are the moral/biographical and religious needs.

g) The last principle is the appraisal of one's spirituality and its components, and the acknowledgment of karma, and the chances/luck of healing from a higher power, God, or spirit in the face of medical helplessness.

On the other hand, spiritual assessment is not a mere talk or a simple recording process, it rather is a process of investigation that searches for what the patient is feeling and thinking through verbal and non-verbal processes for quality of life to deliver meaning and purpose in one's suffering. [3] Moreover, before the spiritual therapeutic assessment in any clinical setting, the assessor competencies in this area need to be aware of the appropriate exploration of some aspects of Advance Care Planning (ACP) like Preferred Priorities for Care (PPC), Advance Decisions to Refuse Treatment (ADRT) and some other related issues. [1]

It is also important for the clinician to acknowledge the risk of terminally ill patient autonomy and social functioning. Social care plays an important role in supporting the ill patient by enabling him/her to connect with his or her community and remove the feeling of being a social stigma. It helps the terminally ill patient to live the life they want and grants them the freedom to have the death of their choice. In the terminal experience, the social assessment is important as it aims to identify the patient's family background and to deliver emotional and social support, which usually improves the patient's condition. Fulfilling the basic social assessment enhances the patient's quality of life until the inevitable death attack. The assessor should be aware of the types of social assessments; Statutory (legal/constitutional) and Specialist Social Care. Statutory care is mostly in practical and physical form that includes support for the caretakers and families, even for the smallest task. On the other hand, Specialist Social Care provides advance care planning, palliative care social support, debt/income maintenance advice, housing, and advocacy support, and most importantly, the pre- and post-bereavement services. [12]

Social care services, being the most important, valuable, and sensitive form of care for quality assessment can be provided by a professional care workforce, and informal carers like families, friends, and volunteers. Moreover, society does need to come together for support and help to meet the demands of the dying individual and have a family that enables someone to die at home peacefully and more meaningfully. However, in the case of those who are alone and without having carers at home or elsewhere, hospitals turn out to be the most likely place of dying. [13] Most importantly, good, and effective communication between physicians, parents, and patients plays an important role in avoiding confusion and misinterpretations of the situation and issues. Information and issues relating to dying and death need to be explored appropriately, sensitively, and in a clear manner. This will help the family and dying patient to have an opportunity for quality time and discussions, saying a proper goodbye, contact relevant people, to prepare themselves for death and bereavement. [15] It is also important to let parents and the community access a maximum number of hours as dying becomes an unpredictable process with numerous possible trajectories depending on a person's circumstances and diagnosis. Thus, death may take years, months, or days from when the condition becomes incurable to end someone's life. Even in the present context of India, people live seven years longer than before but spend 8 years in bad/ill health resulting in experiencing the most vulnerable stage of their life. Therefore, multiple settings of care are required to be delivered in different ways, to meet the patient's needs and help them achieve their specific aspirations, rather than focusing on the medical illness alone. Looking at the emerging needs of the dying patient at present, it is true to say that health and social care services are unlikely to cope with the effects of changing populations unless major changes have been made to the way they are delivered.

Challenges and Conclusion

Modern medicines and technology succeeded in treating and sustaining human life longer than before. However, fail to deliver well-being, quality of life, and a good or peaceful death. Due to the absence of holistic assessment in palliative end-of-life care, India today turns out to be a country not to die for many. Holistic assessment is not only an important approach to care but also the needs of the hours for dying patients. It is a pathway moving from the early identification of the dying phase, through changes in a person's condition and the treatments provided to the last days of one's life. It is the assessment that comprises the patient as a 'whole person' by promoting an appropriate response to the patient's needs in the face of death and dying. The whole person assessment in end-of-life care includes the factors like, physical, social, psychological, and spiritual, which are identified as the important domains of care for the overall health, well-being, and quality of life. It provides the necessary skills that help to fulfill the core principles and objectives of end-of-life care, enabling 'good' and 'meaningful' death. Most importantly, it addresses the underlying issues for the whole person treatment, providing the needs by preserving and respecting the dignity, right for self-determination and the autonomy of the patients and families. However, due to the confusions over its assessment like, who to assess, how, where, why and when to assess, holistic assessment turns out to be the most difficult task in the clinical environment. The confusion is mainly due to the lack of proper education and training among the health care professionals and other care providers in most of the existing medical colleges, institutes, and hospitals in the country.

The unavailability of proper syllabuses like any other popular medicinal medical subjects is also another important reason for not achieving peaceful and meaningful death. The failure of quality end-of-life care in India is also due to the negligence of hiring well-trained psychologists and other social workers in the clinical setting. Though being the most difficult task in clinical settings, holistic assessment in end-of-life care is an important mechanism that comprises the patient as a whole person through promoting suitable responses to the patient's needs in the most vulnerable stage of their existence. Moreover, it is the mechanism of care that brought palliative end-of-life care to a new level of its existence by providing patients and families with the maximum amount of effective and standardized end-of-life care. It also promotes well-being and quality of life in the face of medical helplessness. However, looking at the practical level of current professional medical practices in India, the holistic assessment is still in its infancy. The challenges lie in implementing the objectives and principles of palliative end-of-life care, which were set up by the WHO and other medical organizations for an end-of-life care assessment. Failing the implementation of ACP and other quality assessments like the preservation of patients' dignity and autonomy, India is considered the worst place for dying. Implementation of holistic care assessment as a subject of study in the medical and para-medical academic programs is also the need of the hours.

References

1. NHS-National Health Service. Holistic Common Assessment of Supportive and Palliative Care Needs for Adults Requiring End of Life Care. New York. NHS. http//: www.gmesn.nhs.uk/attachments/article/99/HCA_guide.pdf. Retrieved from the web January 2023.

2. NCPPC-National Clinical Programme for Palliative Care. Palliative Care Needs Assessment Guidance. New York. NCPPC. http//:www.hse.ie/eng/service/publications/ clinical-strategy-and-programes/palliative-care-needs-assessment-guidance.pdf. Retrieved from the web January 2023.

3. Dighe M & Rajashree KC. End of Life Care. Handbook For Certificate Course in Essentials of Palliative Care. Lucknow: Indian Association of Palliative Care. Calicut: Indian Association for Palliative Care, 2011.

4. Rego Francisca & Nunes Rui. The Interface Between Psychology and Spirituality in Palliative Care. http//:www.hpq.sagepub.com. Retrieved from the web November 2022.

5. Christine Kalus. The Role of Psychology in End-of-Life care: A Report Published by the Professional Practice Board of the British Psychological Society. New York. British Psychological Society. http//:www.palliativ.kiev.ua/upload/8.pdf. Retrieved from the web January 2023.

6. Ellershaw John & Ward Chris. Care For the Dying: The Last Hours or Days of Life. BMJ. 2003; Jan; 326 (7379): 30-34.

7. Jennifer et al. Clinical Challenges to the Delivery of End-of-Life Care. The Prim Care Companion J Clin Psychiatry. 2006; 8 (6): 367-372.

8. Kelly Brian, McClement, Susan & Chochinov Max H. Measurement of Psychological Distress in Palliative Care. Palliative Medicine. 2006; 20 (8): 779-789.

9. Kumar T Manoj. Psychological Issues. Handbook For Certificate Course in Essentials of palliative Care. Lucknow: Indian Association of Palliative Care. Calicut: Indian Association for Palliative Care, 2011.

10. Stiefel R et al. Depression in Palliative care: A Pragmatic Report from Expert Working Group of the European Association for palliative Care. Support Care Cancer. 2011; 9 (7): 477-488.

11. Leyla F & Fatemeh A. Understanding the Role of Spirituality and Faith in Relation to Life Expectancy and End of Life Experience in Terminally Ill Cancer Patients. Gerontol & Geriatric Stud. 2017; 1 (4): 1-10.

12. Holloway, Margaret et al. Spiritual Care at the End of Life: A Systemic Review of Literature London. http//: www.dh.gov.uk/publications. Retrieved from the web January 2023.

13. Kellyhear A. On Dying and Human Suffering. Palliative Medicine. 2009; 23 (5): 388-397.

14. Sulmasy P. Daniel. A Biopsychosocial-Spiritual Model for the Care of Patients at the End of Life. The Gerontologist. 2002; 42 (III): 24-33.

15. Ellershaw John & Ward Chris. Care For the Dying: The Last Hours or Days of Life. BMJ. 2003; 326 (7379): 30-34.

CHAPTER – FOUR

The Role of Psychologists in End-Of-Life Care

Abstract

The psychotherapeutic approach to terminal illness can serve as restoration therapy to deliver hope and healing even when a cure is not possible in a terminal diagnosis. It can reform the terminal patient to look at life from a different angle to find the quality of life in the face of inevitable death. Moreover, as psychologists are well-trained professionals to impact other's lives in various ways, they are the right professionals who can effectively deal with the emotional sufferings and mental disharmony of patients with major chronic illnesses like heart disease, cancer, AIDS, Dementia, and Chronic pain. The interventions of psychologists and their biopsychosocial-spiritual psychotherapeutic techniques will deliver a new horizon in Indian palliative end-of-life care through its positive outcomes. Thus, the implementation of the psychotherapeutic approach to terminal care in clinical practices could successfully encounter several psychological issues like depression, anxiety, mental disharmony, and stress that usually occur in the last hour's experience of terminally ill patients. Moreover, the psychotherapy techniques of pain management and relaxation therapy could also be a great help in producing quality of life through quality end-of-life assessment.

Key Words: Psychologists, Psychotherapy, Mental Health, Distressing Pain, and Symptoms.

Introduction

There is no easy way to deliver quality of life for those experiencing the impossibility of a cure for their terminal illness experiences. Especially, in a country like India which is the cantered of world cancer mortality and the highest contributor to the world cancer death at present scenario as per the WHO report. However, palliative end-of-life care's primary aim is to let terminally ill patients experience meaning in illness by any possible means in clinical practices. To enable the patient to have quality of life through quality end-of-life care, and to deliver patient preference treatment. Caring for distressing pain symptoms, feelings of discomfort, emotional suffering, and mental disharmony in a clinical setting requires a maximum number of cares, effort, and attention, which are hardly visible in Indian palliative end-of-life care at present. Most of the Indian clinicians working in palliative end-of-life care failed to possess these requirements in their clinical practices, resulting in terminally ill patients drowning in their emotional suffering and mental disharmony. The miserable conditions of terminally ill patients can be minimized effectively through the deliverance of the patient's psychological, social, and spiritual approaches alongside contemporary medicinal treatments.

The effective implementation of the psychological approach to terminal care can restore patients' hope, quality of life, and patient's anxiety over inevitable death, which usually occurs in the terminal experiences of terminally ill patients. In a country like India, where more than two lakh people die per day without experiencing the quality of life and well-being of the whole, the psychotherapeutic approach to care will successfully encounter several psychological symptoms of a dying patient. Moreover, the psychotherapeutic techniques of pain management and relaxation therapy could be a great help not only to the patients but also to the family and the clinicians that will give a new horizon towards the palliative end-of-life care of the country. The underlying objectives of palliative care do not confine to bodily pain and symptoms treatment alone, rather it seeks for the wellbeing of the whole with quality of life. The whole-person treatment includes physical pain, psychological suffering, social stigma, and fulfilling the spiritual needs of the terminal patient in clinical practices.

The Concept of Psychologists in Palliative End-of-Life Care

Living with dignity is the constitutional right given to every Indian by the law of the country. However, in most of the existing palliative end-of-life care centers in the country, mental disharmony, stress, depression, and emotional suffering were left unconcerned which gave the terminal patients' lives no value. The prime focus in Indian palliative end-of-life care is on physical pain and symptoms, in which the psychological symptoms in terminal experience are not considered as part of terminal illness that leaves the patient in hopeless and helpless conditions. However, as per the concepts of WHO palliative end-of-life care is a specialized area of healthcare given to any terminally ill patient, to prevent unwanted experiences and to relieve the patients from mental and physical pain-related sufferings by any means. However, the core aim which is to produce quality of life through the whole person treatment is sometimes not visible in the clinical practices of the country, mainly due to the absence of a multidisciplinary team. Palliative end-of-life care is a multidisciplinary critical care approach, which serves as a healing therapy for terminally ill patients, in India is provided mainly by physicians alone in the absence of any other care providers like psychologists and social workers, confining mainly to the contemporary medicinal realm alone. However, Irene in "Psychosocial Issues in Palliative Care" stated that in clinical practice meeting the psychological needs of all those involved and understanding the psychological dimension of the work in palliative end-of-life care strengthen the contributions of any professionals with quality care outcomes [1].

To Dawning, palliative end-of-life care is specialized medical care provided at any given point in the trajectory of an illness to alleviate a terminally ill patient physical, psychological, and social sufferings to enhance the quality of life in any possible means. The purpose is to manage symptoms effectively through comprehensive interdisciplinary support given to the terminal patient and family throughout the illness, regardless of cancers of all stages in the clinical practices [2]. Looking at Indian palliative end-of-life care it is visible as a mere medical treatment given to terminally ill patients in a separate ward that requires the activity of physicians alone, in which the involvement of professional psychologists is neglecting to the most. This makes the palliative end-of-life care in the country fail to produce quality of life leaving emotional suffering and mental disharmony untreated, which were the major symptoms of terminal illness, rather than the physical pain symptoms. However, the inclusion of professional psychologists in clinical practices can give the certainty of healing the whole person even when a cure is not possible. It will help the physicians to achieve the best possible quality of life for the patient and family in the best possible ways with quality end-of-life care in the country. The clinician role of psychologists can prevent terminally ill patients from those treatments that violate their preferences, preserving the patient's autonomy, values, and dignity, which will enhance the terminal patient's conditions and well-being by any means through psychotherapeutic techniques [2,3]. Implying the said techniques in the terminal illness treatment policy will create the bringing of a new horizon of care in the country.

The Significance Roles of Psychologists in Clinical Practices

In a country like the UK, Canada, the United States, Australia, and Iceland, professional psychologists play a significant role in palliative end-of-life care alongside clinicians in clinical practices, resulting in producing the quality of life for those with terminal illnesses. At present, in developed countries, psychologists are increasingly in demand in the health care systems, especially when a cure is not possible in the course of an illness. However, the involvement of psychologists in palliative end-of-life care in India is visible and minimal, though the rate of terminal illness in the country is growing rapidly and at present becoming the world's top contributor to cancer mortality.

- Effective interventions of psychotherapeutic approaches to palliative care alongside the treatment of physical pain and symptoms

- Ensuring the psychological well-being of the patient and family by healthcare providers

- Quality psychological assessment to address the complex emotional and mental trauma, which is often experienced by terminally ill patients

The WHO highly emphasizes the involvement of Psychologists in palliative care teams to ensure overall well-being. In palliative end-of-life care, the psychotherapeutic approach to terminal care could be effective mostly before the terminal patient's critical condition strikes, during the terminal diagnosis, even in the advanced stage of terminal illness, and for the bereavement policy as noted by several studies. We are in an era where death is no longer confined to the home atmosphere anymore, it has been institutionalized with several therapeutic techniques in hospitals, old age homes, and other clinical care centers aiming to deliver quality end-of-life care with good and meaningful death. Thus, assisting health care providers by practitioners or clinical psychologists becomes essential to uplift the standard of palliative end-of-life care in the country and to meet the patient's needs and requirements. The Psychologist in clinical practices can play the essential roles of an advocate, counselor, educator, evaluator, and researcher that would enhance the quality of care and treatments. The role of psychologists is not limited to the patients alone, it could effectively manage the terminal patient family well-being conditions and the stressful events of the clinicians through supportive counseling psychotherapy [5,6]. The outcomes of the psychologists in terminal treatments will give the physicians quality treatment decisions, which are in line with the patient's choices, help in adjusting to difficult situations, make the patient emotionally strengthened to face death anxiety, and create awareness for general preparations for death and bereavement policy.

The psychotherapeutic approach to terminal illness and terminal care is a patient preference structure of care in the face of medical helplessness [7]. It is only through psychotherapeutic therapy that acknowledges the patient's nature of distress. It examines the hopelessness and the burdensome experiences caused by terminal illness [8]. When a cure is not possible in clinical practices the psychotherapeutic approach can restore a patient's sense of meaning, hope, value, and dignity usually gives a peaceful death to the patient and helps the patient's family in their bereavement period. Several existing research highlight the psychotherapeutic approach to terminal care as an effective coping mechanism against terminal illness experience of any stage, which helps the patients, and the clinicians avoid having wrong perceptions of cures in clinical practices. The time when clinicians mostly needed psychologists in palliative end-of-life care is mainly when it comes to the patient's mental disharmony and a hopeless experience [9]. Moreover, the care for terminally ill patients demands an extensive amount of care, which the doctors and nurses alone cannot manage effectively. Terminal ill-treatment is not confined to physical pain and symptoms alone; it rather requires several mental and emotional treatments, which are beyond the riches of contemporary medicines and technologies. In terminal diagnosis, psychologists have the professional capability to reduce tense situations through their good communicator and comforter role. Psychologists can also help in building a quality relationship between a patient and the care providers and with the patient's family to come together for meaningful discussion in any possible way regarding patient treatment, plan, and bereavement policy [10].

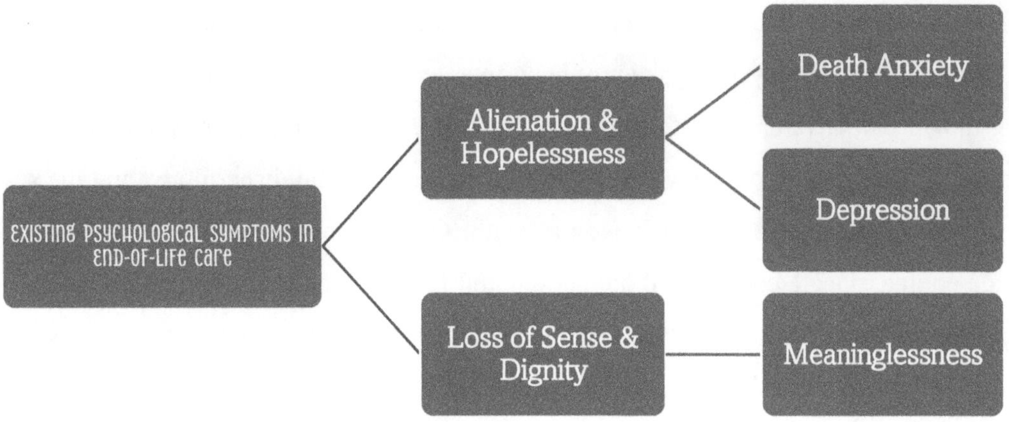

The intervention of clinical or health psychologists in a terminal treatment can help the patient control the physical symptoms and provide a supportive presence to the patient to overcome isolation. It can help the patient to recognize his/her value, meaning, purpose, and reconciliation with self, others, and loved ones. The psychotherapeutic involvement in terminal treatment will help the patient to reframe his/her life goal through self-reflective life review psychotherapy [11]. Thus, psychologists can rebuild and reconstruct the present patient and clinician communication barriers to uplift Indian palliative end-of-life care to new horizons. The involvement of psychologists in the clinical practices of the country could successfully play the role of the patient's guides to perform meditative practice, which will help the patient to focus on the healing of the whole even when a cure is not possible in his/her diagnosis. The psychotherapeutic intervention can provide the certainty of the terminal patient being respected and preserve personal values, which help the patient to view life with a positive, which is still in the condition of limitless achievement apart from being ill. Such therapeutic intervention is what Indian palliative end-of-life care needs, which could give meaning to suffering and will be able to give the two lakhs terminal patients dying per day in the country. However, expert interventions in dealing with disappointment, death anxiety, a sense of hopelessness, and a patient-centered therapy for the meaning-making process are not visible in Indian palliative end-of-life care at present. Thus, failure to access the emotional sufferings and mental disharmony in Indian terminal treatments resulted in worsening the conditions of the terminally ill patient in most cases.

The Indian healthcare system must learn from the British Psychological Society (BPS) concerning terminal ill-treatments and its bereavement policy for effective end-of-life care in the country. In terminal ill-treatment, British Psychologists acknowledge that the terminal experience is preoccupied with several unwanted negative feelings, and loss of sense, and dignity. Not only the patients, but even the clinicians also experience several psychological difficulties in caring for terminally ill patients which becomes a major risk to palliative end-of-life care, which makes psychological problems an essential component in clinical practices [12]. Thus, Indian palliative end-of-life care can only be fruitful and effective when psychologists treat the existing psychological problems like depression, mental disharmony, and the several anxieties that are associated with pending death. Grief psychotherapy and counseling can provide compassionate care toward the patient and family. Moreover, psychologists can help the patient and family understand the confusing medical terms, terminal diagnosis procedures, and the effects of Chemotherapy, and deal with the clinician's stressful moments effectively in clinical practices.

Psychologists are not only effective with patient's depression, and emotional and mental disharmony, but they can facilitate several psychological problems of the 'trio' (patient, family, and clinician) in clinical practices through their biopsychosocial-spiritual psychotherapeutic techniques [13]. The psychologists in the health care systems of the country can play an effective role in researchers exploring several major issues around terminal illness and palliative end-of-life care, which could help in advancing quality health care planning, quality decision-making, and exploring the latest aspects of psychological pain and symptoms management. The involvement of psychologists in the clinical practices of the country can ensure the reliability of palliative end-of-life care on the battlefield against the cool-blooded killer 'Terminal Illness.' With the involvement of professional psychologists in Indian palliative end-of-life care, the terminal diagnosis could see its new horizons within a decade. The process of undergoing the terminal diagnosis and chemotherapy is the time when the patients are overwhelmed with several sentimental crises of living or dying. It is the time when they need psychological intervention the most and the psychotherapeutic approach to care at this point is visible as the most effective mechanism in terminal experience, which the Indian palliative end-of-life care failed to deliver to the terminal patients in the country thus far. This is the reason, India is not a good place to die, where the patient's preference for care is not met, the patient's dignity is unconcerned, and the voice of the drying is not listened. The psychological approach to terminal care and treatment could deliver patient preferences of care, and treatment, help patient to make sense of their terminal diagnosis, can provide social and spiritual services effectively [9]. The psychological intervention could prevent terminal patients from symptoms worsening his/her condition and could help in preventing the terminal patient from a disability of the organ system, which usually occurs in the last hour of terminal experience.

Practical Challenges

Psychologists have great roles to play in Indian palliative end-of-life care while dealing with diseases and their therapeutic process is not an easy task. One reason why psychologists are being neglected in the health care systems of the country is the concept of the people. "Psychologists are not medical practitioners who do not have well-to-do knowledge with contemporary medicines and its trajectories." Such concepts prevail, as the majority of Indians could not differentiate the role of psychologists and psychiatrists in clinical practices—a lack of knowledge about the role and outcomes of psychotherapeutic interventions in terminal illness. At present, it will take a decade or two for India to realize the importance of psychologists and psychotherapeutic techniques in the clinical practices of the country.

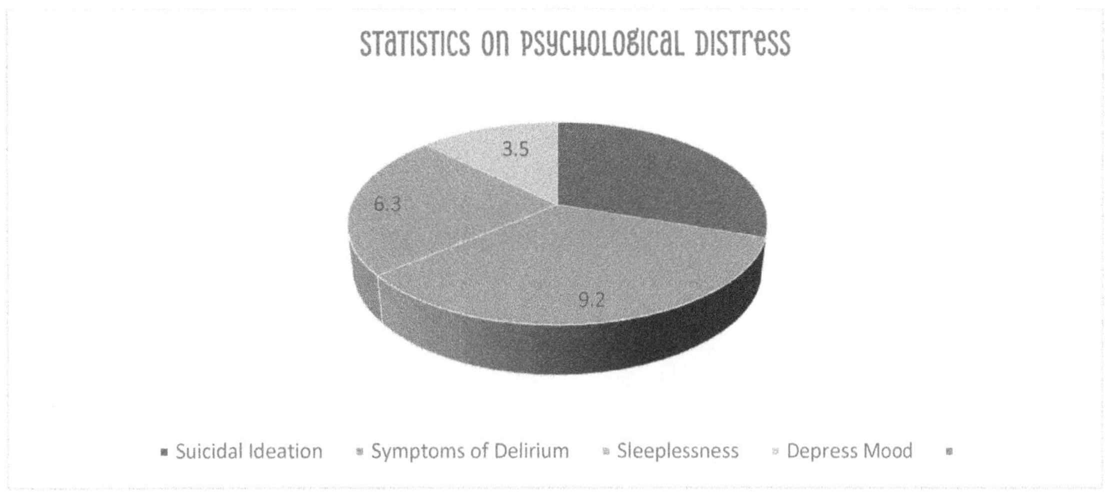

Modern medicine and types of equipment cannot cure symptoms like depression, loneliness, emotional suffering, stress, mental disharmony, feelings of uneasiness, and death anxiety. It needs psychological interventions to treat those psychological symptoms, which usually arise in a terminal patient's experience. On the other hand, Indian psychologists also need to create an awareness platform where they can earn people's trust the same way they trust and rely on other healthcare providers in the country. For effective functioning, psychologists working in the clinical realm need to have basic knowledge of the cause of cancer. What terminal illness is all about? What are the types of symptoms? How is terminal illness diagnosed in a clinical setting? Psychologists involved in palliative end-of-life care need to undergo a basic study of pathophysiology, which is the physiology of abnormal states, especially the functional changes that accompany a particular syndrome or disease. [12] Psychologists need to be aware of the disease processes of the patients they are assisting, mainly on some of the ongoing illness processes like cancer, organ failure, progressive neurological condition and frailty, organ functioning, patient autonomy, and mental clarity, which will enhance their ineffective therapeutic approach to terminal ill patient.

Psychologists should pay attention to the physical and mental well-being condition of the patient, family, and clinicians. The psychologists assisting a terminal patient are required to have some knowledge of the use of opioids, the constitutional laws with regards to terminal treatment policies, and quality medical treatment types, and should be fully aware of the bereavement policy. The clinical assessment of a psychologist does not end with the death of the patient; it rather is an ongoing process until the bereaved family's psychological and physical conditions stabilize. In this therapeutic process, psychologists need to be equipped with several therapeutic techniques and symptom management.

The psychologists are also advised to be aware of the patient's unspoken emotional challenges, which were usually inherited during terminal ill experiences. There is a danger in not treating the patient's unspoken emotional challenges, leading to suicide, and ineffective terminal medication and diagnosis [10]. Psychologists need to have sufficient knowledge of biopsychosocial-spiritual psychotherapeutic techniques and methods to deliver effective psychotherapeutics in clinical practices. It is essential to have the ability to identify a patient's emotional or mood conditions, and desires, and the ability to solve conflict issues or situations in any given context. Psychologists are also required to possess the discerning capability to identify the family and clinician's present condition and the capability to recognize the types of treatment the patient and family want their clinician to perform for effective treatment and fruitful psychotherapy. The challenging role of the psychologists working in the clinical setting is the time when their patients are not in the condition to make his/her decisions and the family members are confused concerning which decision to make for their loved ones. Especially, when it comes to euthanasia, the use of opioids, and other critical conditions, psychologists are mostly required to assist the patient and family for quality decision-making. Therefore, it is essential for psychologists to be wise in their assessment and to be aware of the assessment outcomes before assisting. Psychologists working in palliative end-of-life care need to be aware of the psychotherapeutic assessment provided to patients and families because it is not just a therapy but rather a critical care medicine, which has its side effects like a wrong medical prescription.

Conclusion

Looking at the Indian health care system at present, clinicians mostly neglect the psychological well-being of the patient and family. The attention of the physician is mostly confined to the bodily treatment, which has no concern for the emotional state of the terminal patient. It is also visible that healthcare providers do not give importance to quality talk or meaningful conversation with the patient and family. Moreover, most of the hospital policy is to restrict doctors and nurses towards frequent conversation, and not to be too close with the patient and family in clinical practices. This could be the reason of Indian healthcare providers fail to provide or understand patient mental wellbeing, to produce quality treatment and quality end-of-life care. Another reason is the concept of the Indians towards psychotherapy, the Indian understanding of psychotherapeutics is mostly with the abnormal behavior or patients, in which the normal patient does not approach psychologists, and need not require psychological treatment, which is a wrong concept that existed in the thinking of most Indian. However, changing this concept could bring quality of life with healthy living.

Psychologists and their psychotherapeutic approach to health care have a huge contribution to pain and symptom management. It is a critical medicine that delivers healing in the face of contemporary medical helplessness, which provides mental well-being and quality of life. Psychotherapeutic intervention can also give awareness, especially in the case of terminal or incurable illness experience. It effectively delivers self-compassion, letting patients be aware of the present condition, and what can come. The psychotherapeutic intervention will help the terminal patient to understand the deeper meaning of life through a self-reflective review of one's life and prepare the patient to face the inevitable death with confidence and deliver a peaceful death.

Reference

1. Tanchel Irene. Psychosocial Issues in Palliative Care. CME-Continuing Medical Education. 2003; 12(5): 249-252.

2. World Health Organization. Palliative Care. http://http://www.who.int/news-room/fact-sheets/detail/palliative-care. Retrieved from the web June 2022.

3. Werth J L, Gordon R, Johnson R R. Psychological Issues Near the End of Life. Aging & Mental Health. 2002; 6(4): 402-412. Doi:10.1080/13607860210000007027.

4. Kaut Kevin P. Religion, Spirituality, and Existentialism Near the End of Life: Implication for Assessment and Application. Journal of American Behaviour Scientist. 2002; 46(2): 220-234. https://doi.org/10.1177/000276402236675.

5. Chochinov Max Harvey. Dying, Dignity, and New Horizons in Palliative End-of-Life Care. A Cancer Journal for Clinicians. 2006; 56(2): 84-100.

6. Puchalski C M. Spirituality and End-of-Life Care: A Time for Listening and Caring. Journal of Palliative Care Medicine 2002; 5(2): 289-294.

7. Meador G Keith. Spiritual care at the End of Life: What is it and Who Foes it? NC Med Journal. 2004; 65(4): 226-228.

8. Rousseau P. Spirituality and Dying Patient. Journal of Clinical Oncology. 2000; 18(9): 2000-2002.

9. The British Psychological Association. Division of Clinical Psychology Faculty of Clinical Health Psychology: Briefing Paper No. 27 Clinical Health Psychologists in the NHS. http://www1.bps.org.uk/system/files/Public%20files/DCP/cat-442.pdf. Retrieved from the web May 2022.

10. Backer Angela. Palliative and End-of-Life Care in the Serious and Persistently Mentally Ill Population. Journal of American Psychiatric Nurses Association. 2005; 11(5): 289-303. https://doi.org/10.11 77 /1078390305282209.

11. Haley E William, Larson Dale G, Kasl-Godley, Julia Neimeyer, Robert A, Kwilosz Donna M. The Roles of Psychologists in End-of-Life Care: Emerging Models of Practice. Journal of Professional Psychology: Research and Practice. 2003; 34(6): 626-633.

12. DeAngelis, Tori. More Psychologists Needed in End-of-Life Care. Journal of American Psychologists. 2002; 33(2): 49-52.

CHAPTER – FIVE

Significance of Psychological Assessments in Terminal Ill Diagnosis

Abstract

As a critical medicine, suffering plays a crucial role as terminal ill experiences are always accompanied by several unwanted psychological and emotional sufferings. In the early stages of any terminal illness diagnosis cure becomes the primary concern for both the patient and the family. However, in the face of medical helplessness, a psychological approach to terminal illness becomes essential to effectively deal with pain and non-pain symptoms. It is not a mere philosophical approach to terminal ill experience, but a humanistic approach that provides hope even in the face of inevitable death. The psychological approach to health and well-being becomes more essential as palliative end-of-life care aims to uplift the meaning-making policy and purpose in suffering that contributes to health to many. Though there are no easy ways to deliver well-being of the whole and quality of life, psychotherapeutics is an effective mechanism to deal with existential suffering, stress, loneliness, alienation, and discomfort usually inherited in the process of terminal ill experiences. The therapeutic aim is to minimize the existential issues that accompany the terminally ill experience and act to the best benefit of the patient and family in clinical practices.

Key Words: Mental Disharmony, Stress, Loneliness, Terminal Ill Experience, and Therapeutic Assessment.

Introduction

Terminally ill experience is pre-occupied with several unwanted ill experiences. In the course of illness, the patient usually undergoes several mental disharmony and psychological issues that make life a living hell. Failing to acknowledge the psycho-emotional symptoms in terminal diagnosis greatly affects the patient's health and sometimes it worsens the patient physical ill condition. Health is a multidisciplinary term that consists of the interventions of several medical professional teams including psychologists, unlike the present existing health care system in India that acknowledges the physical pain symptoms alone and leaves the non-pain symptoms untreated. The psychotherapeutic approach to terminal health is a modern humanistic approach that aims at delivering the whole person's treatment through its person-centered therapy for quality of life even in the face of inevitable death. The psychotherapeutic approach has nothing to do with the philosophical approach of Sigmund Freud's psychoanalysis towards psychiatric patients, but a purely goal-oriented humanistic approach to one's illness that addresses the ultimate needs of the dying individual for the well-being of the whole in any given environment. Thus, with an urgent necessity for psychotherapeutic intervention in terminal diagnosis, the present study has been formed to uplift the palliative end-of-life care condition in India into its new horizon.

The Concept of Psychological Approach to Health and Wellbeing

It is the individual confrontation with the existential isolation, fear of death, anxiety, and meaninglessness in suffering that results in inner conflict mainly among those with advanced medical ill experience. The concept of a psychological approach to health is psychodynamic, which is practicable, concrete in its nature of existence, bearing positive impacts, and after all flexible in its approaches. The psychotherapeutic becomes essential as patients experience alienation, the meaninglessness of life, the feeling of being an outcast in society, and mental disharmony in the course of their terminal illness. When those confronted with mental disharmony and psychological symptoms are left untreated, the physical pain symptom treatment mostly produces negative results as mental well-being is the core to patient recovery and healing. [1,2] However, the acknowledgment of distressing pain symptoms turns out to be the most neglected area of care resulting in leaving the terminally ill patients in the most traumatic conditions. The psychological approach to terminal care is a holistic approach that views human illness as associated with his/her biological, social, emotional, and spiritual needs that need special consideration in clinical practices. The fundamental belief of the psychological approach is to acknowledge the isolation, hopelessness, and meaninglessness that patients usually experience in the course of their illness and to inspire the dying individual that they are still in the condition of limitless achievement possibilities. It is also to help the patient realize that they have the freedom to exercise their responsibilities in fulfilling their wishes until the inevitable death strikes. [2,3]

The uniqueness of the psychotherapeutic in terminal experience lies in its phenomenological inquiry toward the dying patient's ill experience by leaving no room for the clinician's personal beliefs, theories, and assumptions. The psychological intervention focuses on encountering the patient's conscious experience and the sub-conscious issues that bother the patient's feelings through its humanistic psychoanalysis. More importantly, it explores and investigates the happening issues and places human experience in its central focus.[4] The aim is to acknowledge the inter-correlation between illness and the social responsibility of a person and to strengthen the individual to face existential challenges through person-centered therapy. The psychotherapeutic approach to existential suffering helps the patient to understand the existential issues that preoccupy the individual and design the methodologies to deal with them effectively in clinical practices.[5] It also serves as a platform that responds to the patient's needs in the face of medical helplessness and explores what it means to be human in the light of limitless possibilities. Moreover, in working with the dying patient the psychotherapeutic approach to care helps in delivering the patient's self-awareness, freedom, and responsibility associated with illness, the search for meaning in suffering, and effective coping mechanism against death anxiety and psycho-emotional challenges.[6]

The Significances of Psychotherapeutic Approach of Care in Terminal Ill Diagnosis

Palliative end-of-life care is an interdisciplinary approach to focuses on pain and non-pain symptom management and to deliver the quality of life through any possible means until the inevitable death strikes a worldwide phenomenon in clinical practices. Psychological assessment is the key factor that plays an important role in dealing with patients' physical discomfort, distressing pain and non-pain symptoms, emotional suffering, and quality decision-making. [7,8] However, the psychological approach to care is an alien term in the Indian medical setting, while in some regions it existed as a merely theoretical approach. On the other hand, the acknowledgment of the psychological dimension of care in clinical practices among the clinical staff will enhance the quality of health care in the palliative care unit. In developed countries, psychologists are placed at the forefront to help the psycho-emotional needs of patients, families, and healthcare professionals in the clinical setting. Looking at the nature of its existence chronic illness, cancer, dementia, and respiratory ailments demand extensive amounts of care and support, in the intervention of psychotherapy has been seen as an effective mechanism with an extensive number of positive outcomes. The inclusion of psychologists helps in examining the psychological consequences of the disease, treatment policy in the patient's best interest, and releasing several built-up tensions along the disease continuum. [9,10]

Moreover, with the recent development of the biopsychosocial-spiritual model of medicine in terminal ill diagnosis, psychotherapeutic intervention becomes imminent mainly to deliver the quality of life for the dying individual and their loved ones. The evolution of psychology to health science helps the terminal patient to explore a sense of hope and gives a sense of comfort, and certainty of being respected and valued until they die. It restores the sense of dignity as being human apart from being with a terminal illness and delivers a peaceful death with meaning in it.[11] Moreover, it's a worldwide phenomenon that there could be no palliative end-of-life care without the psychological approach to care and it satisfies the meaning of what it means to be a good palliative care. The psychological intervention gives the patient a supportive presence during several existential sufferings, helps in controlling physical pain symptoms, helps in recognizing purpose in life through systematic life review, reframing life goals with limitless possibilities, and helps the patient to focus on healing in the face of medical helplessness. However, failing to acknowledge those unwanted feelings like the sense of hopelessness, burden to others and loved ones, and loss of will to live, will result in worsening patient physical ill condition and sometimes lead to suicidal activity. [10,11]

The psychological approach to care is a person-centered therapy deeply rooted in human existential theory and practices; the mechanism that brings awareness about death and dying that makes every act count. The therapy gives the patient a desire to live in the face of death anxiety, isolation, and inner conflicts through the courage to face the existential challenges and commitment to human responsibility towards his/her choices. Alongside the addressing of the patient psycho-emotional issues, the psychotherapeutic also helps the individual to embrace what life gives and to live courageously with curiosity. The prime focus of the therapy is to explore patient choices, the 'why' of living, and the ability to do away with despairs and burdens. Most importantly the sense of ownership over life and death through its person-centered and meaning-making psychotherapy. [6,9] The therapy also serves as a guiding mechanism for the patient to live more authentically in relationship with life by taking responsibility for their choices that have the advantage of hindsight. The therapist on the other hand does not impose their personal beliefs, but rather acts as a guiding factor that accompanies and builds quality relationships between the patient and the clinicians. The authenticity of psychotherapy lies in the fact the therapist is a human who experiences existential sufferings and psycho-emotional challenges with a prime focus on uplifting the patient's conditions through a transformation experience and delivering a quality of life. It focuses on the inter-correlation and intrapersonal nature of human existence that has no room for the philosophical dimensional approach to human existence in its clinical practices and respect human personal values, beliefs, and human limitation. In another sense, wounded healer therapy recognizes the existence of inner conflict within the self through its humble approach of healing and being healing. [10]

The difference between philosophy and psychology lies in the fact that the psychotherapeutic approach to illness is to uphold that everything in life has a meaning in it, meaningless is the process in which the meaning has not been discovered yet. The psychological approach to illness and suffering prioritizes the search for meaning in every human circumstance and humans could self-discover and reflect upon their existence. Thus, the underlying principle of its therapeutic approach is to promote the patient's authentic relationship with self, others, and the world and to promote self-awareness of responsibility and liberation over life, feelings, and choices. Psychotherapy aims to liberate oneself from the captivity of their circumstances and to make one responsible for their life through active participation against existential challenges. [14,15] However, In the face of inevitable death and suffering finding meaning and purpose is never an easy task that requires specific skills and techniques in clinical practices. The psychotherapeutic approach enables the terminally ill patient to accept what had already happened and helps them to create a new worldview that gives creative ways of living with an illness alongside the psycho-emotional challenges. Even in the face of the crisis of emotional instabilities, dysfunction, and death anxiety, it is the psychotherapeutic model of care that embraces the individual condition as it is and gives a different worldview of life, which has meaning and purpose in it. [4,13] The therapeutic aim is to let patients experience freedom of choice over life and death, to widen the clinical domain by allowing the interventions of the socio-spiritual assessment, and to acknowledge the neglected areas of care in its clinical practices to produce quality life and wellbeing of the whole. Thus, the therapy helps minimize existential anxieties and create a platform where the dying individual can construct a new worldview that suits them the best.

Challenges

At present, the role of psychologists and their psychotherapeutic approach to care barely exists in the academic realm alone in most cases. The involvement of the psychological approach to terminal care is mostly misunderstood with psychiatric treatment and is not an option even in the patient's choices of the treatment policy, due to its unavailability in its clinical practices. Terminal ill diagnosis is always a crucial moment for the patient and the family that requires the whole person treatment which includes emotional suffering, mental disharmony, and psychological symptoms to deliver quality of life for the patient and the loved ones. Yet, the prime focus in Indian terminal diagnosis mostly deals with the physical pain symptoms alone while leaving the non-pain symptoms untreated. The reason could be the absence of a psychological approach to care in the curriculum of oncologists and other clinicians. On the other hand, if effectively implemented, as a critical medicine it could serve as a healing therapy and the meaning-making policy in the face of medical helplessness, but the minimal availability of clinical psychologists in its clinical practices is of the greatest concern. The core emphasis of the psychological approach to terminal care is to make patient realizes the awareness that they are in the possible condition of limitless achievements, to find meaning in suffering, and to understand the deeper meaning of life that serves as an effective coping mechanism when cure is not possible. Psychotherapy is an effective tool to deal with patients' mental disharmony and emotional sufferings and to make the patient utilize their limited leftover time in the most productive ways.

Moreover, in a country like India, which is a hub for terminally ill patients the psychological approach to care is the need of the hour. The immediate challenge is to implement the psychological domain of care in the training of clinicians and the involvement of psychologists in the terminal diagnosis. Spreading awareness on the importance of the psychological dimension of care in terminal diagnosis and it has nothing to do with the psychiatric treatment among the people is also an emerging challenge in India today.[13] The minimal availability of palliative care centers with maximum needs is also another great concern.

Conclusion

The needful task is to implement proper policy and structure of care of palliative end-of-life care and the participation of well-trained health or clinical psychologists in its medical team for quality assessment and positive health outcomes. Meeting the needs of the dying individual places the psychotherapeutic approach to the terminally ill becomes the patient-preferred care as found by much experimental research and the therapy that delivers healing as an alternative to cure in clinical practices. Not only the patient and the family, but the therapy also enables the clinician working in the palliative care centers to be mentally and emotionally prepared during a hectic environment. The therapy also extends its domain and works effectively even in the bereavement period and enables the loved ones to have a sense of recovery from their loss.

References

1. Suantak D Vaiphei and Devendra Singh Sisodia. Psychotherapeutic Intervention in Terminal Diagnosis: An Overview. Journal of Indian Health Psychology, 2018; 13 (1): 20-34. ISSN:0973-5755.

2. Diamond Stephen A. What is Existential Psychotherapy? www.psychologytoday.com/ blog/evil-deeds/201101/what-is -existential-psychotherapy. Accessed on March 2, 2022.

3. Good Therapy. Existential Psychotherapy. www.goodtherapy/types/existential-psychotherapy. Accessed on February 9, 2023.

4. Spinelli, Ernesto. Existential Psychotherapy: An Introductory Overview. Analise Psicologica. 2006; 3 (XXIV): 311-321. DOI: 10.14417/ap.170.

5. Boston Patricia, Anne Bruce, Rita Schreiber. Existential Suffering in the Palliative Care Setting: An Integrated Literature Review. Journal of pain and Symptom Management. 2011; 41 (3): 604-618. DOI: https://doi.org/10.1016/j.jpainsymman.2010.05.010.

6. Yeolekar ME, Mehta1S, Yeolekar A. End of Life Care: Issues and Challenges. Journal of Postgraduate Medicine. 2008; 54 (3): 173-175. DOI: 10.4103/0022-3859.41795.

7. National Health Service. Holistic Common Assessment of Supportive and Palliative Care Needs for Adults Requiring End of Life Care. gmesn.nhs.uk/attachments/article/99/HCA_guide.pdf. Accessed on November 27, 2022.

8. Kasl-Godley Julia E, King DA, Quill TE. Opportunities for Psychologists in Palliative care. American psychologist. 2014; 69 (4): 364-376. Doi: 10.1037/a0036735.

9. Haley E William, Larson Dale G, Kasl-Godley, Julia Neimeyer, Robert A, Kwilosz, Donna M. Roles of Psychologists in End-of-Life Care: Emerging Models of Practice. Professional Psychology: Research and Practice. 2003; 34 (6): 626-633. DOI: 10.1037/0735-7028.34.6.626.

10. Rousseau P. Spirituality and Dying patient. Journal of Clinical Oncology, 2000; 18 (9): 2000-2002.

11. Deurzen-Smith E Van. Existentialism and Existential Psychotherapy. www.researchgate.net/publication/265245397_existentialismandexistential_psychotherapy. Accessed on December 20, 2022.

12. Ackerman Courtney. Existential Therapy: Make Your Own Meaning. Positivepsychologyprogram.com/existential therapy. Accessed on February 12, 2022.

CHAPTER – SIX

Understanding the Psychological Symptoms in End-of-Life Care

Abstract

The concept of psychological depressive symptoms affecting terminally ill patients still stood as a mystery in many clinical practices. The psychological traumatic and depressive stressors are the factors responsible for destroying the quality of life and affecting the terminally ill individual in the most degrading ways. Alongside the physical pain symptoms, the terminal illness experience is always accompanied by several unwanted mental disharmonies and emotional suffering like toxins, mood disorders, trauma, and low self-esteem. The higher level of stress and depression determines the growth of tumors and cancer metastasis rate in any terminal diagnosis. This assesses the psychological non-pain symptoms essential alongside the physical pain symptoms. Failing to acknowledge the patient's traumatic experience and depressive stressors will make the treatment unproductive and increase suicidal activities.

Key Words: Depression, Stress Experience, Traumatic Events, and Quality of Life

Introduction

Terminal illness in its nature of existence is a traumatic event with stressful experience, resulting in developing the highest psychological depressive symptoms. Unlike any other ill diagnosis, the psychological depressive stressors in terminal ill experience worsen the individual physical pain symptoms and increase tumor growth rate into its advanced stages in the most fruitful ways. It is essential to understand the tumor types to deal effectively with the patient's stressful and depressive symptoms in clinical practices. Several research findings suggested that it is not the tumor or pain symptoms alone that destroyed the patient's hope and well-being. It is instead the depressive stressors that completely disturb the unique peaceful environment. Thus, understanding the psychological non-pain symptoms alongside the physical pain symptom treatment will better understand the patient's cognitive process with the stressors and its behavior outcomes in any terminal diagnosis.[1]

Stress and Depression in Terminal Ill Experience

Though advanced medical science technologies effectively address the wide-ranging needs of terminally ill patients, it is mostly confined to the patient's physical pain symptoms alone. Terminal ill diagnosis, unlike other illnesses, requires a whole-person treatment that acknowledges the psycho-emotional sufferings that affected the patients in the most degrading ways. Terminal illness is accompanied by several unwanted experiences that hugely disturb the individual's well-being and quality of life. Some of the stressors that preoccupy terminally ill patients are trauma, anxiety, loss of will to live, and other mental disharmonies that serve as the underlying threat to patient quality of life and well-being.[1,2] Among all the factors, death anxiety is the main contributing factor affecting the patient's immune system, unhealthy relationships, loss of sense of self-esteem, and poor decision-making towards treatment plans and policy. The psychological stress and depression associated with the initial stage of cancer and its metastasis hugely decrease the patient's quality of life and well-being. Stress in its nature of existence is an adaptive reaction in cancer metastasis that usually produces physical, mental, and behavioral changes in a patient's terminal experience. It is a non-specific psychological reaction towards life situations' external and internal demands beyond the average human ability to deal with, killing the brain cells. Comparatively, stress is visible as the most common experience among terminally ill patients with long-term psychological distress.[2] In one of the latest findings, depression and stress are the two everyday unwanted experiences among cancer patients in India (n=320; 72.5%).[3] Depression is higher in the age group of 18-40 among the women with breast cancer patients in India (n=270; 96.7%).[4] Depression, on the other hand, is more than just a feeling of worthlessness or mood disorders; it is a symptom that is linked with human brain chemicals of serotonin and norepinephrine, which causes several pains like joint and back pain with sleep disorder and can even lead to a depressive episode. In the World Health Organization's (WHO) latest report, depression accounts for patients with a physical disability, and mental and behavioral disorders patients of all ages.[5]

Depression and stress are the two most common psychological disorders among terminally ill patients in India. It decreases the patient's health stability, and heightened self-depreciation, reduces energy, and is different from grief. The underlying features of depression that terminally ill patients usually experience include bipolar disorder, clinical depressive disorder, persistent depressive disorder, and seasonal affective disorder. The degree of depression varies from the individual experiences, and it has no age bar. The recent findings in India concluded that depression is higher among terminally ill women patients than the men group.[6] In another latest study among cancer patients in India, the depression rate ranges from 4.4% to 89.9%, emphasizing emotional distress. The rate of depression increases as per the stage of the cancer metastasis. On the other hand, lack of awareness, ignorance, social stigma, and discrimination become the underlying factors for worsening the patient's mental health conditions. Depression has no age bar and is hugely responsible for suicidal activities, which India is considered the most depressed country in the world. Some of the most depressive symptoms are loss of appetite, loss of self-esteem, energy, concentration, and slow cognitive process.[7]

The genetic and biological factor plays an essential role in a patient experiencing depression and stress. Specific genes increase the risk of developing a mental illness, depending on one's life situation, which may trigger it like abuse or trauma (life experiences). Some mental health issues arise through the parents' environmental exposures resulting in the child's mental disorder. Exposure to environmental stressors, inflammatory conditions, toxins, alcohol, and drugs while in the womb can sometimes make the child suffer from mental illness. Brain chemistry is also another cause of mental health problems; when the neurotransmitters that carry signals from one part to the other parts of the brain and body are impaired, nerve receptors and nerve systems change dramatically, leading to depression and other emotional disorders.[8] Cancer/terminal illness is a unique experience with both the disease and the situational challenges that produce uncertainty over life and huge psychological effects that disturb the individual nature of existence most rigorously. It is essential to acknowledge the adaptive patient capacity over their environmental challenges and understand how the individual responds to the stressor's events in terminal experience. Knowing the level of the patient's sense of sensitivity towards the stressors event is also essential in developing the coping strategies most effectively. Looking at the current condition of India, the depressive stressors that put the individual life into miserable conditions and severe problems in daily life and relationships remain unconcerned. Moreover, the signs and symptoms of depression can vary depending on the individual's mental or psychological state. In general, mental health symptoms can affect emotions, behaviors, and the cognitive process.[9]

Assessment of Psychological Stress and Depression in Ene-of-Life

Psychological stress, anxiety, and depression are the most common adverse outcomes in any terminal experience, which require special consideration in attending to the patient emotional needs and mental problems through effective coping strategies in clinical practices. Coping is an ongoing process that needs several cognitive efforts and energy to deal with the depressive stressors; it requires skills and techniques to give the terminally ill patient the ability to adjust and overcome the environmental challenges or reduce the stressors events in life. Though the levels of depression and stress differ in terminally ill men and women, the coping strategies don't differ, in the two most effective coping mechanisms are social support and problem-solving techniques. In dealing with depressive stressors, studying the patient's past and present history is essential for practical problem-solving, decoding, and addressing the stressors in the most effective and appropriate ways. The hypothalamic-pituitary-adrenocortical axis (HPA) and the sympathetic-adrenal-medullary (SAM) system of the human organs responsible for mood disorders and negative feelings demand special assessment in palliative end-of-life care. [10, 8]

The HPA and SAM influence the effects of stress in cancer metastasis and have several disease risks related to physiological processes, affecting immune cells' activity, including natural killer (NK) cells, T cells, and macrophages as the outcomes of activating the stressful stimuli. In dealing with psychological stress, the involvement of family and friends to give emotional support to the patient is the best coping mechanism to fight against the immunological and endocrinological consequences of the patient's psychological functioning. It is also visible that psychosocial-emotional supports are an effective mechanism in reducing tumor metastasis and associated symptoms. It serves as the factor that controls the degree of anxiety and depressive stressors that regularize the individual peripheral and central nervous system functioning in the most effective ways. Immuno-modulatory therapy is also an essential assessment in dealing with patient depressive stressors symptoms in clinical practices. [11,9] Psychotherapeutic intervention is more effective than psychotropic medicines for patient recovery from depression and well-being. Moreover, the mere use of counseling therapy alone without psychotherapy has minimal impact on dealing with the depressed situation of the terminal patient. Person-centered therapy with a holistic approach to terminal care can successfully encounter psychological distress stems, and emotional needs, reconstruct mental stability, and build practical coping skills. The early intervention of psycho-stimulant substances like dextroamphetamine or methylphenidate is also a well-recognized therapy against insomnia and hugely improves patient mood and well-being.[12]

The intervention of the psychological approach to terminal care has been visibly effective in three essential dimensions for patient quality of life; in effectively reducing the psychological depressive stressors, increasing the patient survivor period, and decreasing the cancer metastasis rate. The collaborations of psychotherapy and psychopharmacological approaches to terminal care are also effective in reducing the tumor growth rate and boosting the immune system's functions.[13] The following are the standard existing measuring scales to effectively measure the level of stress and depression in terminal ill diagnosis:

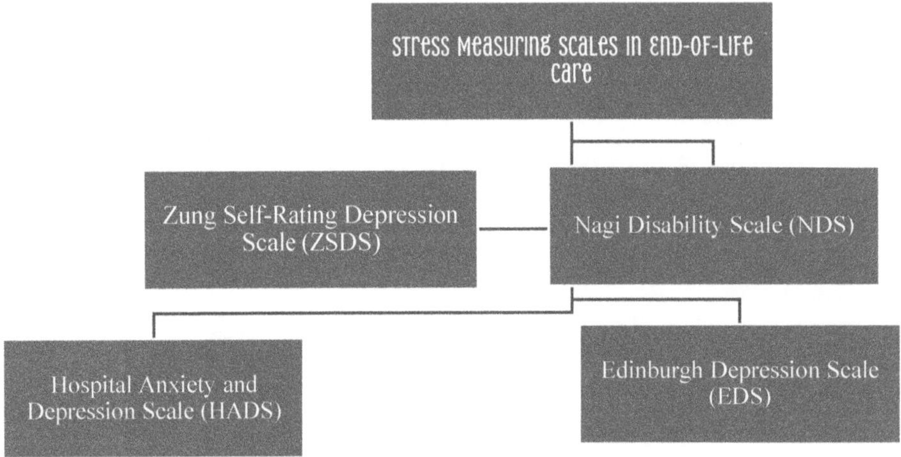

The Hospital Anxiety and Depression Scale (HADS) is a fourteen-item scale depression rating tool used to indicate the antidepressant medical response, while the Zung Self-Rating Depression Scale (ZSDS) is a twenty-item self-reporting depression measurement scale used to show the presence or absence or the level of depressive symptoms in palliative end-of-life care patients. The Edinburgh Depression Scale (EDS) is a ten-item postnatal depression tool used to measure symptoms like guilt, hopelessness, mood swings, and other related cognitive processes in a terminally ill patient. The Nagi Disability Scale (NDS) is the clinical instrument that identifies the degree of psycho-emotional suffering and other associated issues among cancer survivors. The Patient Health Questionnaire (PHQ-2) is used in screening cancer patients for undiagnosed depression. It is effective in screening larger groups of patients for depression. [8,9]

The use of verbal screening instruments by forming some relevant questionnaires regarding the low and high mood of a patient undergoing depression can also enhance the treatment policy to address depressive stressors. According to DSM-IV (Diagnostic and Statistical Manual of Mental Disorders), depression is mainly associated with a patient's loss of interest in daily activities, difficulty in making a quality decision, psychomotor agitation, and suicidal motive because of the disease effects, in which the psychological symptom of depression is seen as the main characteristic of its outcomes. Thus, the early initiation of psychological treatment within an adequate period needs to be assessed. If the depressive symptom of hopelessness is not addressed in its early period, it can easily combine with the grief response that usually causes the loss of specific abilities in the patient's terminal experience. The primary concern of the clinician should be adequate control over pain and symptom management and other disease risks in advanced patient illness and to prevent the patient from certain depressive disorders through any possible means.[10] Most importantly, the assessment should be regular, including the appropriate time and place, intensity, and quality of evaluation. It is also essential for the clinician working in palliative end-of-life care to identify the difference between physiological tolerance, physical and psychological dependency, and pseudo-addiction in assessing the patient.[12]

Suggested Coping Strategies

Among all the effective coping mechanisms against stress and depression in terminal ill experiences, drawing a positive attitude to self and the given environmental challenges by accepting the life situations beyond control and adjusting is the most effective coping mechanism for those with terminal ill experience. Striving towards self-esteem and learning to relax over sensitive issues, rather than being aggressive towards what life brings. Adopting the habit of regular physical exercise, managing a balanced diet, avoiding things that create sleeping disorders, and abstaining from the excessive use of alcohol and other related drugs are the core factors to eliminate stress and depression and maximize the quality of life by minimizing depressive stressors.

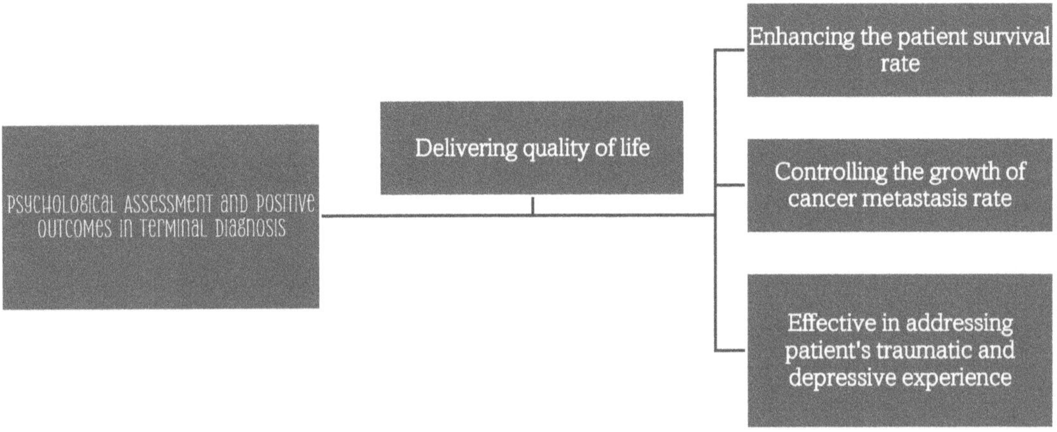

Diagnosis with cancer/terminal illness is a challenging experience filled with anxiety, negative feelings, and mental disharmony, yet understanding the kind of tumor involved, its metastasis, treatment policy, and the side effects would help in creating appropriate coping skills and the ability to deal with it in the most un-harmful way. Knowing the cultural and religious background is essential for every clinician, as in some cultures, death and dying are taboo and have no place for public discussion.[11,12] Preserving patient autonomy by respecting the choice of the patient about the disease risks information and the inclusion of the patient in the decision-making management team is also essential to produce a quality of life in end-of-life care. Honest conversations between the patient, clinicians, and the family on the disease and treatment outcomes can serve as the platform where all the people involved in end-of-life care can come together for effective plans and policies to encounter the environmental and psychological challenges in patient terminal experiences.[13]

There is no better-coping mechanism than the early interventions with proper treatment plans and policy in dealing with the terminal illness diagnosis. The involvement of family loved ones, and the community inpatient terminal experience is the best coping mechanism to meet environmental demands like traveling, having quality time together, and creating good memories. The life review method is another coping mechanism that helps the patient set new life goals, which have the maximum possibilities to achieve before the inevitable death strikes.

Assisting the patient in managing their financial income for treatment expenses through any possible means can serve as a contributing factor to improving the patient's quality of life and well-being in clinical practices. Forming a small cell group within the cancer-affected community, including cancer survivors, to discuss their experiences, insights, and feelings, about any terminal illness is another effective strategy to fight against cancer stigmas. [4,5] Some effective psychotherapeutic coping mechanisms are given below:

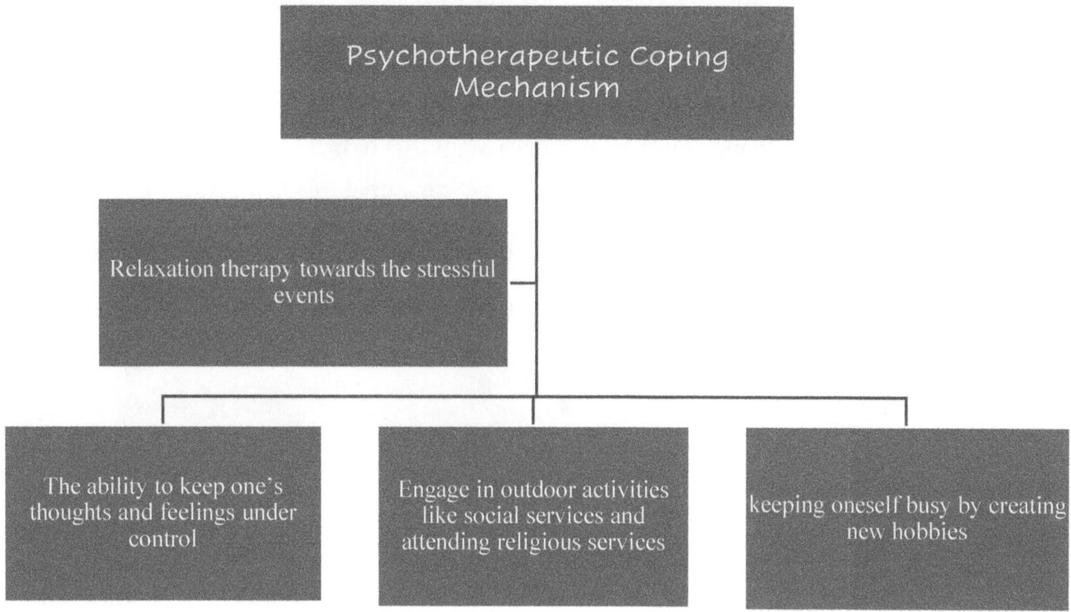

A spiritual coping mechanism is a modern humanistic approach to dealing with stress and depression in the face of medical helplessness. Spiritual psychotherapy is a modern holistic approach to illness in health and medical sciences, which serves as an effective coping mechanism against several unwanted experiences like existential stress, anxiety, depression, and emotional suffering that pre-occupied the terminally ill patient in terminal diagnosis. When cure becomes uncertain in terminal diagnosis, spirituality becomes part of the patient's existence, potentially communion with self, others, nature, and the transcendent being. It is the coping mechanism that delivers the whole person's treatment by addressing the patient's self-identity, inner peace, reconciliation, and hope with gratitude, which provides healing even when a cure is impossible in a terminal diagnosis. The involvement of psycho-social therapy is another effective coping mechanism that enables the dying individual to connect with the society where they belong. The treatment makes the patient experience the feeling of being valued by eliminating the existing social stigma of being an outcast.[13,14] However, the absence of anti-anxiety, anti-psychotic, and mood-stabilizing therapeutic approaches to terminal care in the current healthcare system in India and other neighboring countries like Nepal, Bangladesh, Pakistan, Myanmar, etc., cancer/terminal patients undergo several unwanted feelings without any quality assessment. Due to the unavailability of whole-person treatment in the country's health care system in general and in the medical curriculum, psychological stress and depression remain untouched in its clinical practices. Thus, India is considered a country not to die by many.[14]

Conclusion

Psychological stress and depression destroy the patient's peace of mind and possess the ability for cancer metastasis growth in the body parts and to disable the organs. The interplay between the environmental challenges, stressors, and the patient's socio-economic, cultural, and religious background needs special consideration in cancer diagnosis to produce the quality of life and well-being of the whole clinical practice. Developing positive mental health and a healthy lifestyle is the core of coping with psychological stress and depression in any terminal experience. Even in the terminal stage when a cure is not possible, finding purpose and meaning in life can benefit self and others and is also an effective coping mechanism to overcome mental health problems.

Reference

1. Deimling Gary, Kahana B, Bowman FK, Schaefer Michael L. Cancer survivorship and Psychological Distress in Later Life. Psycho-Oncology. 2002; 11(6): 479-94. DOI: 10.1002/pon.614.

2. Tan Siang Yong, Yip A. Hans Selye (1907–1982): Founder of the Stress Theory. Singapore Med J. 2018; 59 (4): 170–171. Doi: 10.11622/smedj.2018043.

3. Vedprakash Sharma, Sunil Choudhary, Mona Srivastava, T. B Singh, Ravi Shankar. Prevalence of Depression, Anxiety and Stress among Cancer and Chronic Kidney Disease Patients. International Journal of Health Sciences & Research. 2019; 9(4): 1-6.

4. Debasweta Purkayastha, Chitra Venkateswaran, Kesavankutty Nayar, and UG Unnikrishnan. Prevalence of Depression in Breast Cancer Patients and its Association with their Quality of Life: A Cross-sectional Observational Study. Indian J Palliat Care. 2017; 23(3): 268–273. Doi: 10.4103/IJPC.IJPC_6_17.

5. Annie Alexander, K Sreenath, R Srinivasa Murthy. Beyond numbers – Recent understanding of emotional needs of persons diagnosed with cancer. Indian Journal of Palliative care, 2020; 26(1): 120-128.

6. Cohen, S. Kessler, RC. Gordon UL. Strategies for Measuring Stress in Studies of Psychiatric and Physical Disorder: A Guide for Health and Social Scientists. New York: Oxford University Press, 1995.

7. Krohne, H.W. Individual Differences in Coping. Handbook of Coping: Theory, Research, Applications. New York: Wiley Publications, 1996.

8. Myrthala Moreno-Smith, Susan K Lutgendorf & Anil K Sood. Impact of stress on cancer metastasis. Future Oncology. 2010; 6, (12): 1863-1881. Doi: org/10.2217/fon.10.142

9. McEwen BS. Protective and damaging effects of stress mediators. New England Journal of Medicine. 1998; 338 (3):171-179. DOI: 10.1056/NEJM199801153380307.

10. Lloyd-William Mari. Difficulties in Diagnosing and Treating Depression in the Terminally Ill Patient. Postgrad Med Journal. 2000; 76 (899): 555- 558. Doi.org/10.1136/pmj. 76.899.555.

11. Reiche Edna M et al. Stress, Depression, the Immune System, and Cancer. The Lancet Oncology. 2004; 5(10): 617-25. DOI: 10.1016/S1470-2045(04)01597-9.

12. Lloyd-Williams Mari. Depression—the hidden symptom in advanced cancer. J R Soc Med. 2003; 96 (12): 577–581. Doi: 10.1258/jrsm.96.12.577.

13. Widera E and Block Susan D. Managing Grief and Depression at the End of Life. American Family Physician. 2012; 3 (1): 259-264.

14. Groninger H and Vijayan J. Pharmacologic Management of Pain at the End of Life. American Family Physician. 2014; 90 (1): 26-32.

CHAPTER – SEVEN

Psychological Aspect of Pain and Symptom Management

Abstract

The concept of pain differs from individual personal physical, emotional, social, and cognitive-behavior conditions. Pain in its nature of existence is a complex psychoneurotic syndrome that requires a multidisciplinary inclusive approach to deal with complicated disorders. Psychological issues are a central concern in dealing with pain syndrome, resulting in maximizing emotional outbursts and disabilities. The immediate context of occurrences hugely influences the perception of the intensity of acute pain syndrome. The cognitive-behavioral psychotherapeutic approach effectively addresses the nature of total pain in the context where it occurs and the associated factors. The pain syndrome needs to be applied by understanding specific components associated with pain and through the optimal comprehensive assessment interventions at a multidisciplinary level. The psychopharmacology aspect of pain management in conjunction with the patient's primary needs is a productive assessment method with several positive outcomes.

Key Words: Assessment, Pain, Coping Mechanism, Distressing Symptoms, and Disorders

Introduction

"We must all die. But that I can save him from days of torture is what I feel is my great and ever-new privilege. Pain is a more terrible lord of mankind than even death itself."

- J.J. Bonica.

Being in pain is a stressful, complicated, and multifactorial experience that destroys individual cognitive and behavioral functioning in dealing with pain symptoms. These psycho-emotional feelings depict the level of pain that maximizes the level of anxiety, stress, and depression. Pain is the one factor that proves the direct link between the human mind and body. The perception of pain demands different understanding paradigms in defining and seeking multidimensional approaches through multidisciplinary team interventions in clinical practices. Pain is not confined within the bio-medicinal realm alone; it is a wide-ranging phenomenon that requires holistic assessment. There are multiple layers of complex thoughts and feelings in the human brain that construct the level or the amount of pain a person experiences and can tolerate. Since it is the human thoughts and feelings that determine how the individual deals with pain symptoms, controlling personal perception and emotion can serve as an effective coping mechanism to modify and cope with the physical pain symptoms.[1] Thus, understanding the psychological aspect of human pain and symptoms could significantly enhance patient treatment and deliver quality of life.

Psychological Distress and Physical Pain Symptom

Pain is the factor that ruins everyday behavior interrupts all activities and is more than a sensational experience. It is a complex component of both physiological and psychological responses in the individual experience. Pain is an unpleasant combination of human sensory and emotion that damages tissues, brain, and memory functioning. The pain symptom demands regular comprehensive assessment to identify the patient physical, psychological, social, and spiritual dimensions through multidisciplinary team interventions for psychodynamic and neurotic assessments. The perception of pain is an individual response to factors like childhood experience, socio-cultural, and heredity that usually produce different aspects of pain and suffering. Pain becomes more severe and unbearable, mainly for those with a distressing socio-cultural group of people. In contrast, the pain thresholds were at a lower rate among the socio-culturally stable group of people with faster recovery rates.

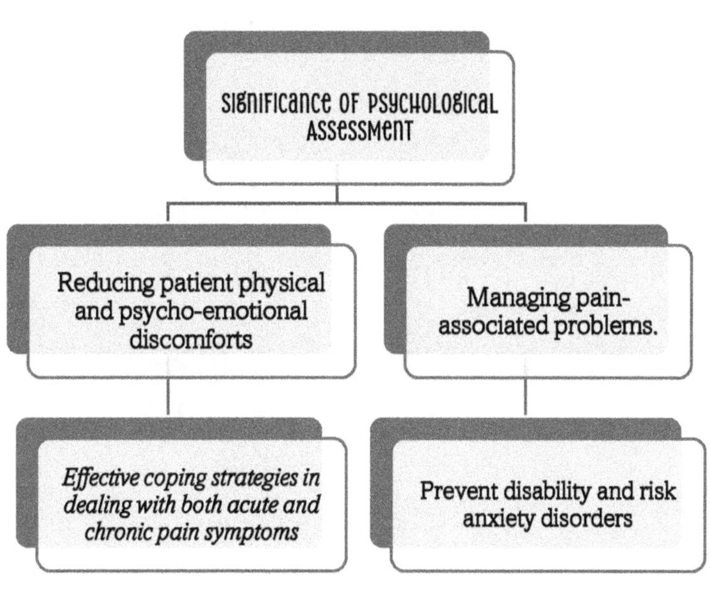

The context of pain and the behavioral condition of the patient also hugely determine the severity perception of pain experienced by the individual, which requires cognitive and practical aspects of psychological care assessment to the earliest.[2] In all the existing ill-related experiences, pain is the underlying source that produces disability and risk anxiety disorders leading to several suicidal activities. Several studies recognize that pain intensity in its nature of existence is in connection with psychological symptoms. The longer the duration of pain, the higher intensity of mood disorder, depression, and anxiety increase the level of pain symptoms. The fMRI (Functional Magnetic Resonance Imaging) mainly depicts how pain symptoms influence mood disorders and emotional aspects in clinical practices. Most research findings stated that psychological depressive symptoms and pain frequency are the two determining factors of human health. The epidemiological evidence also affirms the high intensity of psychological distress over pain symptoms among medically advanced ill patients. The ovarian hormones are also equally responsible for pain intensity in different regions of the human brain/mind state.[3]

Thus, understanding the individual concept of physical pain is essential to understanding the endurable pain level and developing effective coping strategies in dealing with both acute and chronic pain symptoms. Chronic pain accompanies several psychological and mood disorders that usually destroy patients' peace of mind and quality of life in their nature of existence. The factors responsible for the causes of chronic pain in the human body are nerve fiber dysfunction through injuries or surgery, patient medical condition, some portions of brain neuron dysfunction, through accident or illness.[4]

Another finding suggested that the immediate context of occurrences hugely influences the intensity of acute pain syndrome. Thereby, if the individual is preoccupied with existential fear and anxiety, even opioids and other related drugs are visibly less effective. It instead worsens the intensity of physical pain syndrome. A recent experimental study also found the feeling of hypochondria or somatic visible in increasing the intensity of physical pain symptoms. On the other hand, timely addressing the pain syndrome by distracting the patient's thoughts with another interest is an effective coping mechanism that reduces the sensitivity rates of pain and suffering.[1] Pain is a distressful and prominent symptom that affects 75-78% of patients with advanced medical illness. It is also evidence that 68% of deaths due to stroke have experienced pain and symptom disorders. The study also depicted that pain syndromes highly affected the individual ways of life, physical functioning, concentration, increasing disease risks, and helplessness. Being in pain is a stressful event that makes the psychological factors central to the individual experience of pain and for quality treatment policy. Stress is the contributing factor for health problems and chronic pain, including blood pressure, heart disease, obesity, and diabetes, and triggers muscle tension that maximizes pain intensity. The treatment procedure demands the associations of the sensory, cognitive, emotional, behavioral, and environmental factors that need immediate assessment in the possible ways for effective pain management.[5]

The Psychological Aspects of Pain and Symptom Management

Despite the advanced modern medical science and technologies in clinical practices, psychological distress remains the underlying issue in dealing with chronic pain. The intensity of psycho-emotional grief associated with pain increases disease risk rates in the individual experience and reduces inpatient quality of life. Pain in its nature of existence is a complex psychoneurotic syndrome that requires a multidisciplinary inclusive approach to deal with complicated disorders. Effective total pain management hugely depends on the holistic assessment of the patient's physical, psycho-emotional, social, and spiritual aspects. Identifying psychological distress-related symptoms and the significant examination of factors associated with pain-related distress are the two essential elements to be identified in pain assessment. Identifying the patient's pain frequency and the amount of pain accounted for health variables is also equally crucial as it significantly differs from the individual cognitive-biological and environmental context.[6] Thus, psychotherapeutic interventions inpatient total pain management become an essential coping mechanism in reducing the intensity of pain. Psychological assessment is also visible in identifying and understanding the patient's negative thoughts, emotional sufferings, and other associated ill behavior, which usually produces discomfort and increases the pain the patient experiences. Pain syndrome needs proper assessment by understanding specific components associated with pain and through the optimal comprehensive assessment interventions at a multidisciplinary level. The psychopharmacology aspect of pain management in conjunction with the patient's primary needs is a productive assessment method with several positive outcomes.[5]

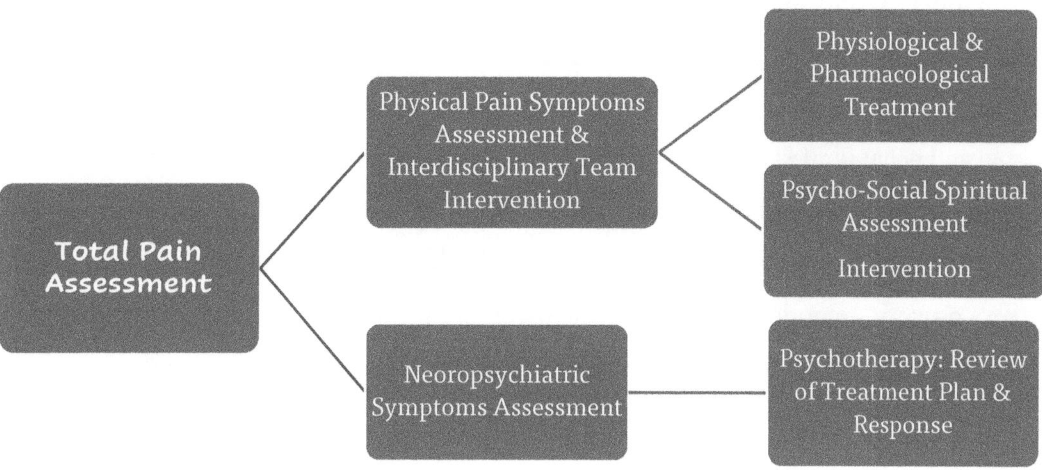

Figure – 2: Total Pain Assessment

On the other hand, recognizing the role of psychologists in pain management began during the 1950s and 1960s with the rapidly growing problems of patients experiencing disabilities through constant chronic pain. On the other hand, the patients were not able to explain the extent of damage caused in their daily experience with the pain symptoms. In finding the nature of pain that interrupts the individual cognitive function, the clinicians focus on biomedicine asper and ignore the psychological factors accompanying the pain syndrome. Failing to acknowledge the psychological components results in long-term psychological damage and makes the pharmacological treatment ineffective.[8] In addressing the total pain, it is essential to understand the context and the factors involved. Cognitive-behavioral psychotherapeutic is the one approach that effectively addresses the nature of real pain in the context where it occurs and the associated factors. Cognitive Behavior Therapy is a humanistic approach that constructs unique coping skills through several relaxation techniques for managing and controlling the total pain symptoms. It adopts diversion techniques against the psychosocial-spiritual signs that accompany the patient's physical pain through its positive therapeutic approach. The therapeutic assessment effectively manages specific body functioning, brain waves, stress response, relaxing muscular tension, and reducing the overall body response to pressure.[9] Acknowledging the patient's socio-cultural background, economic status, and belief system is another critical area to be identified to deliver quality treatment procedures in total pain management.

The biopsychosocial model is a modern humanistic approach that incorporates patient sensory, cognitive, emotional, behavioral, and environmental factors in understanding and managing pain symptoms. Mainly for adults with chronic pain, the cognitive-behavioral model is an essential coping mechanism for relieving pain and recovery from symptoms. The study on pain experience among the medically ill population found that pain is due to patient psycho-emotional and behavioral factors like beliefs, fear, and addiction to drugs. In addition to chronic pain, most of the patients experience physical organ dysfunction, sleep disorder, fatigue, isolation, and care assessment dissatisfaction. The side effects of pain hugely affect the patient's cognitive process, emotional outbreak, and other phobic responses. It requires the psychological understanding and assessment of patient pain experience alongside the bio-medicinal supports for effective pain management in clinical practices. On the other hand, the psychosocial approach is the model of care that encounters environmental challenges and other inevitable cognitive issues in chronic pain experience. A pilot study done on chronic pain management shows the increasing reliability of the psychological instruments used to treat patient cognitive-behavioral therapy towards chronic pain. The treatment aims to reduce the patient's maladaptive behavior, beliefs, and negative thoughts and identify those associated harmful components that make pain treatment ineffective. The therapeutic assessment helps in re-organizing the patient's cognitive process through pain therapists, anesthetists, clinical psychologists, and physiotherapists in clinical practices. The pain management medicinal contents differ as per the patient's perception of the pain and cognitive-behavioral context. It is based on seven fundamental principles: Direct positive reinforcement of pain behavior, Indirect positive support of pain behavior, Positive reinforcement of good behavior, Physical fitness and function, Cognitive reframing, Education and empowerment, Critical process factors, and evidence-based. [10,7,8]

Challenges and Discussion

The emerging issues in pain and symptom management are opioids and other related drugs that lead to addiction or total dependency. This addiction and total dependency make the psychological intervention more essential to control the dependence or total reliance on opioids and other drugs through its non-drug psychotherapeutic techniques. The patient mainly develops total dependence on drugs in chronic pain when their psychosocial-emotional sufferings are not identified and treated on time. On the other hand, chronic pain is a stressful event, subjective experience, self-limiting but not self-evident, which becomes the underlying public health concern. To encounter frustrating patient events and difficult situations effectively demands multimodal approaches to care with multidisciplinary team interventions. No doubt that humans are destined to die, but the pain is a terrible lord rather than death itself. So, saving the individual from the torture of pain and its side effects becomes the core concern for the multidisciplinary teams involved in clinical pain management.[11] However, in a country like India, distressing psychological symptoms are still considered as symptoms not to be treated in its clinical practices. Painful patient symptoms and emotional suffering are not considered an illness to be treated in most cases. It is only through identifying and acknowledging the psychosocial-spiritual distressing symptoms associated with pain, that the influential 'total pain' management policy can be successfully implemented. The holistic assessment in clinical practices is satisfactory for the patient and is a rewarding activity even for the health care professionals.

The war against chronic pain symptoms remains a difficult one in clinical practices. It always co-existed with several psychologically distressing symptoms, which sometimes result in a patient physical disability. Albert Schweitzer wrote: "The use of narcotics in terminal cancer is to be condemned if it can be avoided. Morphine and terminal cancer are in no way synonymous. Morphine usage is an unpleasant experience for most human subjects because of its undesirable side effects. Dominant in the list of these unfortunate effects is addiction."[12] The psychological non-drugs therapeutic approach is the only way to relieve pain that prolongs suffering without addiction and zeroes adverse side effects. Pain management is a unique challenge to health care professionals that requires several sensible and pragmatic diagnostic approaches to intervention, alongside quality management skills and strategies.[12] At present, realistic expectations, and recognition of the limitations in chronic pain medication are the two emerging challenges in chronic pain management. The use of opioids is another fundamental challenge to every healthcare professional. The dangers of opioids and other related drugs can be mainly visible in worsening a patient's ill condition, loss of memory, untimely death, and maximizing tension if overprescribed. It requires an appropriate pain management policy and comprehensive strategies that work in the patient's best interest with the minimal inclusion of the use of opioids or total avoidance of opioids and other related drugs. Pain management strategies should optimize effectiveness with minimal adverse side effects through the psychological mind-body therapeutic approaches. The primary aim of chronic pain management is not to eradicate the pain, but instead to help the patient adjust its thresholds through appropriate care interventions.[13]

In chronic pain management, the patient and even those clinicians addressing the pain symptoms experience several psychological disorders like stress, stigmatization, isolation, and being disturbed in their everyday lives that require special considerations. Thus, psychological issues become the central concern in dealing with pain symptom management in clinical practices. It is to be noted that improving the pain management standards will inevitably enhance the patient/clinician's quality of life and well-being of the whole in any clinical practice. The psychological cognitive-behavioral therapeutic approach is the existing effective model of care to encounter the complexity of pain experience through its biofeedback and relaxation therapy. It is essential to establish a patient referral model to pain clinics, financial support, acknowledge patient attribution, and consistently evaluate patient treatment outcomes or progress in pain management. Patient physical fitness also plays a vital role in managing pain-related symptoms that can provide patient self-reinforcement with a positive outlook toward environmental challenges. Some of the underlying factors that need to be evaluated in psychological pain assessment are care goals, present/past adherence to diagnosis/prognosis, patient beliefs, and cultural background. Comorbidities and related symptoms apart from the pain syndrome, patient history of drug consumption, ongoing patient cognitive functioning with the treatment, and socio-economic status are also essential.[14]

The clinicians should be cautious in differentiating between the patient's physiological tolerance, physical and psychological dependency on opioids, and related drugs in pain assessment. The number of medications for pain control and the negative phenomenon after the withdrawal of drugs is an important domain that requires special consideration. Psychological assessment is another critical area of care to help the patient develop the ability to create self-defeating and self-denigrating insights to encounter reality and pseudo-addiction behaviorism. It will also help enhance the individual capability of stress management to undergo effective self-relaxation therapy that will lead the individual to identify and solve their problems. Psychological assessment is also visibly effective in reforming or improving the daily habits of the patient's physical activity by not allowing pain symptoms to take over individual happiness. Developing a healthy lifestyle, distracting pain through social integration, and engaging with newly formed hobbies are also an essential coping mechanism against pain syndrome. [14,7] The psychological aspect of pain management is a growing public health concern that identifies the patient's pain frequency to establish a quality treatment plan and policies. The psychological cognitive-behavior and evidence-based strategical therapeutic approaches are effective with chronic pain of every age and complex cultural background. The psycho-spiritual model is also another effective pain and symptom management mechanism, mainly for those with psychological depressive symptoms through chronic pain. [15 Thus the underlying factor in pain management is to acknowledge both the mental and physical risk factors for effective pain management strategies. The concept of total care approaches that address patient socio-economic and other bio-environmental challenges through multidisciplinary team interventions could effectively help the patient in their pain experience more than any other method.

Conclusion

Pain is a stressful, complicated, and multifactorial experience. It is a universal symptom that disturbs the whole process of normal human organ functioning. Whether acute or chronic pain it is always accompanied by several unwanted, ill feelings that increase the disease risk. Psychological assessment is a safer approach to care that provides a non-drug method that directly deals with the origin of pain symptoms. It helps reduce the psychological depressive stressors that worsen the individual pain and cope effectively with several factors associated with pain and suffering. Thus, learning how to cope with the problems and stressors related to pain and suffering is the core criterion for effectively dealing with the pain symptoms.

Reference

1. George R. Hansen, George R & Streltzer, John. The Psychology of Pain. Emerg Med Clin N Am 2005; 23 (1): 339–348. Doi:10.1016/j.emc.2004.12.005.

2. Meldrum ML. Pain: Physiology and Psychology in Encyclopedia Britannica. https://www.britannica.com/science/pain. Accessed from the web on December 17, 2019.

3. Gorczyca R, Filip R, Walczak E. Psychological Aspects of Pain. Ann Agric Environ Med. 2013; Special Issue (1):23-27.

4. Intermountain Healthcare. Pain and Symptom Management. https://intermountainhealthcare. org /services/hospice-palliative-care/services/pain-and-symptom-management. Accessed on December 18, 2019.

5. Rizk Dahlia. Palliative Care: Pain Management. https://www.cancertherapyadvisor. com/home/decision-support-in-medicine/hospital-medicine/palliative-care-pain-management/. Accessed on December 18, 2022.

6. Baker, T.A., Krok-Schoen, J.L. & McMillan, S.C. Identifying factors of psychological distress on the experience of pain and symptom management among cancer patients. BMC Psychol 20i6; 4 (52): 1-7. Doi:10.1186/s40359-016-0160-1.

7. Eccleston C. Role of psychology in pain management. BJA: British Journal of Anaesthesia 2001, 87 (1); 1:144–152, https://doi.org/10.1093/bja/87.1.144.

8. APA. Managing Chronic Pain: How psychologists can help with pain. managementhttps://www.apa.org/helpcenter/pain-management. Accessed on December 19, 2022.

9. Zara, C, Baine, N. Cancer pain and psychosocial factors: a critical review of the literature. Journal of Pain and Symptom Management 2002; 24:526–542.

10. Turk DC, Rudy TE. Neglected factors in chronic pain treatment outcome studies—referral patterns, failure to enter treatment, and attrition. Journal of Pain 1990; 43 (1): 7–25. DOI: 10.1016/0304-3959(90)90046-g.

11. Bonica J. J. History of pain concepts and therapies. 1990: 2–13. In Thomas MA. Pain management - the challenge. Ochsner Journal 2003; 5 (2):15–21.

12. Thomas MA. Pain Management - The Challenge. Ochsner Journal. 2003; 5 (2):15–21.

13. Harvard Medical School. Challenges of Managing Chronic Pain. https://www.bmj.com/content/356/bmj.j741. Accessed on December 22, 2022.

14. Groninger Hunter. Pharmacologic Management of Pain at the End of Life. American Family of Physician 2014; 90 (1): 27-32.

15. Lee, Y., Wu, C., Chiu, T. et al. The relationship between pain management and psychospiritual distress in patients with advanced cancer following admission to a palliative care unit. BMC Palliat Care 14 (1): 1-7. Doi:10.1186/s12904-015-0067-2.

CHAPTER – EIGHT

The Art of Break Bad News in Terminal III Diagnosis

Abstract

Most patients appreciate facts about their health, but for the clinicians breaking bad news is one of the most difficult tasks in palliative end-of-life care, but a must in clinical practices. It requires special skills and the ability to deliver bad news without hurting the sentiments of the patient and the loved ones. Many clinicians working in palliative care are incompetent in handling the process of delivering bad news, mainly due to the lack of effective communication skills, and sometimes are preoccupied with fear and nervousness. A time of breaking bad news is the most crucial moment when the dying individuals are mostly accompanied by several negative feelings and emotional breakdowns, which require a good structure manner and design techniques to put forward. Yet few of its skills and techniques are known among the medical practitioners in their medical curriculum during their training period. Delivering bad news requires clinicians' advanced preparations on how much information the patient and the family would like to acquire, a quality therapeutic relationship, and being emotionally well-prepared. The challenges lie in breaking bad news an important domain in terminal diagnosis, but the clinicians are mostly not aware of how, when, and where to deliver in its clinical practices which usually creates a communication gap between the clinicians and the patient.

Key Words: Breaking Bad News, End-of-Life Care, Communication, Emotional Feeling

Introduction

In End-of-Life Care, nothing is more crucial than the time of breaking bad news to the patient and family. It is the time when the patient and loved ones feel an emotional outburst with several distressing outcomes. The time they are mentally unstable and need multiple care assessments in clinical practices. Even for those clinicians working in palliative end-of-life care, breaking bad news is something that preoccupies them with fear and nervousness. Breaking bad news is the least pondered topic of discussion in Indian medical colleges or Institutions. However, the physicians are oblique to deliver the bad news regardless of clinician-patients-family emotional status. It is a crucial moment that requires effective communication skills and techniques to communicate with the dying individual and family in the most appropriate ways. The immediate challenges lie in how well the clinicians prepare the clinical environment before delivering the bad news. It is also important for clinicians to be well-prepared mentally and emotionally. Yet, death and dying at present are still taboo in many Indian cultures. Thus, in breaking bad news in such a context the clinicians need to be cautious on how to break the bad news most effectively without hurting the emotional sentiments of the patient and the family.

Importance of Breaking Bad News in Palliative End-of-Life Care

Bad news in terminal illness is the time when the medical scientific findings declare that the disease is incurable and is always undesirable for the patient, family, and even for the clinicians. In general understanding, bad news is any piece of sensitive information that can affect the peaceful environment of an individual, in which the harm that can be caused to the one who receives is unpredictable as it depends on the degree of bad news the information contains. It is the way the individual responds to the bad news that determines the degree of damage caused and hugely depends on personal psychosocial-emotional health status. The characteristics of the bad news always harm the recipient, and in what ways it harms the individual is of the greatest concern. The disease is the leading factor that causes death; however, inappropriate deliverance of the bad news is also equally responsible for shortening life for those with acute advanced medical illness.[1] The clinicians on the other hand are also oblique to preserve the autonomy of the patient in any circumstances and the patient has the right to know or ignore the information with regards to their ongoing treatment. A good clinician is the one who acts in the best interest and benefit of the patient. They acknowledge and respect the patient's intention without forcing them to let them know about their treatment plan, policy, and outcomes.

Clinicians possessing the ability of effective communication can ease half of the burden of breaking the news, and comfortably deal with patients and their families. Building a quality relationship with the patient and family will help the clinicians with how to deliver the bad news without hurting their feelings. It is also essential for the clinician to be mindful in addressing the queries about the patient's treatment policy and emotional stability.[2] Socio-cultural and religious background awareness of the patient is also an important domain for the clinician. As in some Indian cultures, death is still a taboo that is not an issue to be discussed in a public setting. The clinicians are not only oblique but delivering bad news most appropriately is the fundamental principle of any health care working in palliative end-of-life care. It is the time when the patient and family are overwhelmed with several emotional breakdowns; they need people to assess their emotional needs the most.[3] It is also the time when the clinicians working in palliative end-of-life care need to assist the patient and the family most effectively and help them build up their self-determination to battle against the inevitable death.

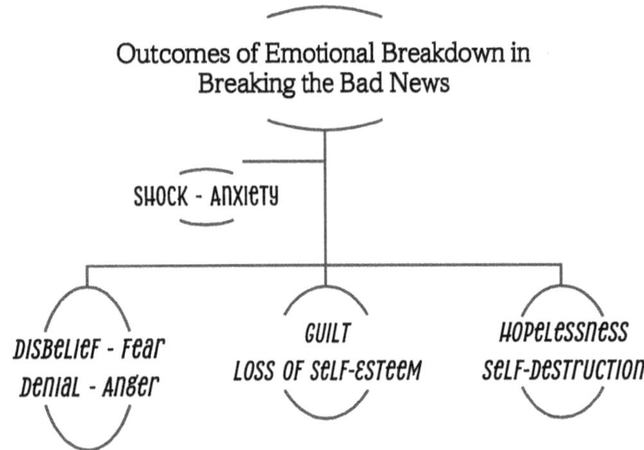

The clinician on the other hand should be aware of the patient's over-dependence on the clinical assessment and other drugs to do away with their emotional pain and suffering. However, the wishes made by the patient in such a crucial situation need to be respected and fulfilled through any possible means. A good clinician is also one who has a thorough check-up on the patient's socio-cultural and religious background before delivering the bad news, which would prevent several unwanted misunderstandings in the clinical practices. It would also help with adequate additional preparation and a quality backup plan.[4] For the majority of medical practitioners, breaking bad news is one of the most difficult oblique tasks one has to perform to fulfill quality assessment. The study found that 72% of Clinicians (Physicians/Oncologists/Nurses) consider breaking bad news as the darkest hours in their clinical practices. Another 65% of the Clinicians have not undergone any proper training in delivering bad news and bereavement policy. However, withholding the bad news from the patient and the family for fear of its negative impacts is considered a serious crime in any clinical practice. Whether good news or bad news, the patient has the full right to know about their disease and treatment details under any circumstances. The primary goal is to make the patient understand and acknowledge self-acceptance and to do the best one can to reduce risks of patient self-destructive outcomes after breaking the bad news. Before breaking the bad news, the procedure should be well framed in an orderly manner that includes the individual concerned, a brief background check on the individual, and other psycho-emotional status.[5]

The clinician responsible for breaking the bad news is required to have communication skills, alongside obtaining the latest information about the patient's ill condition and treatment policy. Inappropriately communicating the bad news could have immediate and long-term consequences for the patient and the loved ones in several ways. On the other hand, withholding the news after getting the concern from the patient is another case. It requires a special training procedure for every clinician involved in palliative end-of-life care, alongside their medical knowledge. Being aware of the proper strategies and skills with compassion is of great importance in breaking bad news.

Principles of Breaking the Bad News

Looking at the current medical practices in India as a whole, the negative emotional outcomes of breaking bad news are of the least concern. Compassionate care for the dying individual is considered out of the box, apart from the clinician attending to the physical pain symptoms. Breaking bad news is indeed becoming a mechanical process that doesn't need any awareness of the strategies, plans, and protocols to follow. In a recent interview, the clinician working in the oncology department stated that "for any clinician, the most difficult task to handle is the breaking of the bad news as it is bad news when the patient and the family expected to hear some good news from the physician.

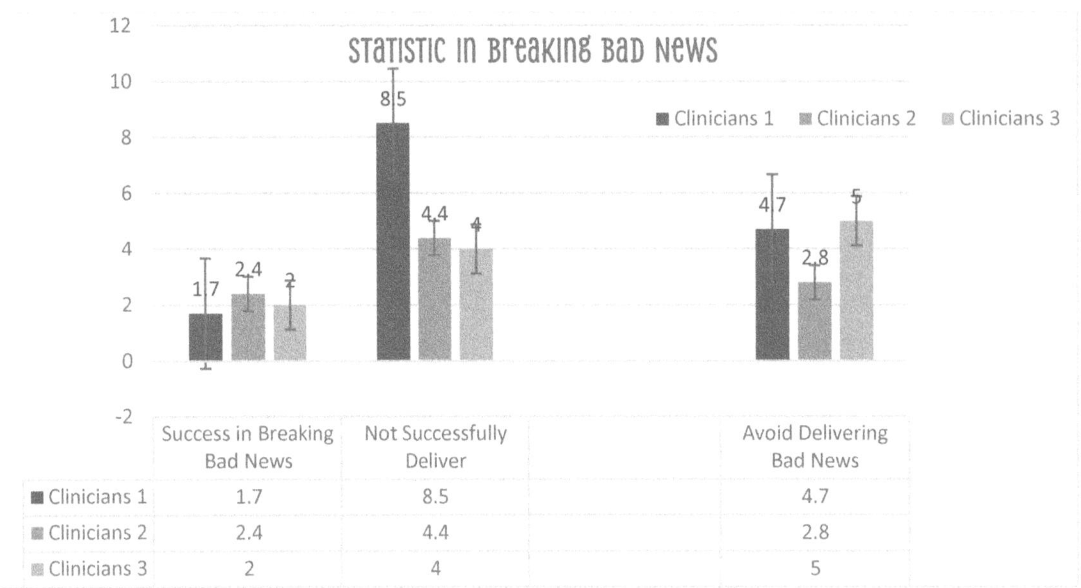

	Success in Breaking Bad News	Not Successfully Deliver		Avoid Delivering Bad News
Clinicians 1	1.7	8.5		4.7
Clinicians 2	2.4	4.4		2.8
Clinicians 3	2	4		5

Figure – 2. [3.4]

In some cases, after a long period of treatment and building up quality relations, most clinicians are afraid that the deliverance of bad news could destroy the patient-clinician relationships. On the other hand, apart from physical pain symptom management, the clinicians were not trained properly on how to handle the psycho-emotional issues of the patient and family. In breaking bad news clinicians should be aware of the guiding principles to break the most sensitive news in the most appropriate and effective ways in clinical practices. They also need to be aware of the first-hand up-to-date information of the patient, to inquire about patient choice with regards to receiving or not receiving the bad news. To what certain degree of information the patient would like to know about his/her condition and to find out to whom the bad news be delivered or consulted? [7]

Challenges are visible to the patient and the family feels disbelief and frightened if the news becomes unexpected. Therefore, by being sensitive, clinicians are responsible for creating an environment where the patient's incurable condition should not be surprising or unexpected. The way how bad news is delivering largely responsible for patient psycho-emotional outcomes and sometimes it can worsen and shorten the patient's physically ill condition. Thus, effective communication in Palliative End-of-Life Care becomes the core component in breaking bad news.

1. *Since breaking bad news is a skill there is a need for establishing therapeutic relationships to obtain the necessary information. It is also important to discuss the diagnosis, prognosis, and treatment options/plan as per the patient/family's convenience to deliver quality end-of-life care.*

2. *Building a good relationship with the patient/family will bring trust, which is the core of quality of care. Without trust the patient can't disclose his/her ill experiences regarding their hope, dreams, values, beliefs, and other important matters, resulting in receiving the unwanted treatment intervention.*

3. *Good communication skills will enable the clinician to demonstrate effectively in responding to the needs of the dying patient/family and be able to break the bad news without hurting the feelings.*

4. *Language use in end-of-life communication has a significant role in breaking bad news. It is important to check and re-check the language used to avoid false hope and not to destroy the hope of the dying individual.*

5. *In end-of-life decision-making, cultural, and religious issues need to be dealt with sensitively as they shape an individual mindset and thinking pattern.*

There is no alternative to the clinician being prepared well emotionally, psychologically, and mentally before breaking the bad news. Another principle to follow is the clinicians inquire whether the patient obtains any information about his/her ill condition by asking some questions relevantly related to the ongoing treatment. Since palliative end-of-life care is not only for the patient, but also important for the clinician to update the latest information about the patient's condition and treatment policy to the family and the loved ones regularly, only if they are interested in knowing the detailed information. However, creating a suitable environment and preparing the patient and family is of the greatest concern, in which the information given should be in plain language by avoiding the use of medical terms that would be difficult to understand and in a systematical way. Even after the delivery of the bad news, the clinician should make himself or herself available to answer the queries of the patient and the family. [3,8] Leaving those queries unanswered or avoiding discussion after the breaking of the bad news will hugely affect the psychological, emotional, and mental domains of all those involved. In dealing with the bad news in terminal diagnosis it demands the assessments of the multi-disciplinary team to make the bad news a part of the ongoing treatment updates, to make the patient feel confidential and comfortable in its clinical practices. At some point, the patient would appreciate it if the clinician frankly told them the truth about their diagnosis, however depending on how much of the information they would like to hear from their physician. [7] Moreover, a good clinician accompanies the patient to address his/her psychological needs, emotional suffering, and mental disharmony that usually occurs after the breaking of the bad news. It is the time when the patient needs someone with whom they can share their inner thoughts, feelings, and their plans. A good clinician also maintains the patient's privacy and comforts the family during their bereavement period.

There is a time when the news is understood, but unable to digest it and finding hard time to accept the truth that they are dying with no option. This is the time when the multi-disciplinary team's immediate interventions in assessing the patient and family are required the most with sympathy and a comforting spirit to help them get through it. The negative impacts of the bad news differ from one patient to the other as per their circumstances. The terminal patient with great expectations for the future like having ambitions, goals, and plans usually has greater emotional outbursts and severe psychological issues. It is effective communication skills with quality follow-up strategic planned techniques that serve as an effective mechanism to encounter patient psycho-emotional issues. [5, 3] The ability of attentive listening, giving an accurate amount of information, and checking whether the given information's where understood are also some of the important principles to be followed in breaking the bad news. However, amid busy schedules in clinical settings maintaining the common principles is one of the challenges that every clinician encounters. The SPIKES [9] procedure is one of the effective models for dealing with bad news in clinical practices.

SPIKES

- Setting
- Perception
- Invitation
- Knowledge
- Emotions and empathy
- Strategy and summary

Breaking bad news is a skill, and not at all easy. Most clinicians have trouble when required to deliver bad news. Bad news is always bad news, however, how it is conveyed can have a profound effect on the patient, family, and clinicians. Another common principle to follow in breaking bad news is the ABCDE model of clinical practices, which does not only focus on setting up the environment but also gives a warning shot before communicating the bad news.

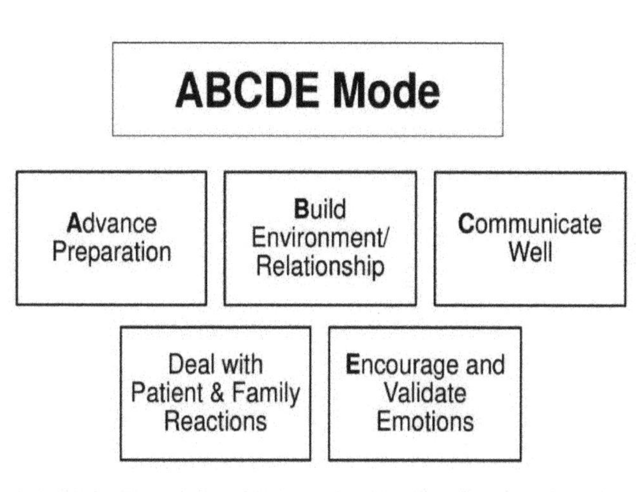

Rabow MW, Mcphee SJ, Beyond Breaking the bad news: How to help patients that suffer West J Med 1999;171:261

Offering *Encouragement and Validate Emotions* with the help of the interdisciplinary team assessment is another effective practice. [1] A recent psychological experiment on breaking bad news among terminally ill patients shows that negative factors like anxiety, fear, stress, and loss of peace of mind are frequently experienced after hearing the bad news. It is very clear that among all the barriers to breaking the bad news in clinical practices, a strong sense of emotional outburst is considered the greatest challenge clinicians working in palliative end-of-life care encounter. Despite the ongoing challenges the survey also claims that the maximum number of clinicians doesn't have the privilege to undergo proper training during their regular medical training period. [10] In most cases, language is also one of the leading barriers to delivering bad news, which will sometimes lead to misunderstanding through miscommunication. The socio-cultural and religious differences between the clinicians and the patients are the most common barriers in the clinical setting. Lack of group discussion among the clinicians on how, when, and where the bad news is delivered is also another emerging challenge that needs proper attention.

Challenges and Conclusion

Breaking bad news is a skill and not all can handle it like any other task. It is always unexpected and shocking, resulting in scattering the thoughts and feelings of both the patient and family. At present, the underlying barriers in Indian palliative end-of-life care could be visible in the minimal availability of clinicians and the increasing number of terminal patients. Thus, delivering a quality treatment could not be possible in the Indian clinical setting, mainly due to the time factor. In the context of Indian end-of-life care, breaking bad news and delivering effective communication is an unheard topic, due to the absence of holistic care in its clinical setting. Effective communication can be empowered only by allowing it as a part of medical academic programs or syllabi at the graduate and post-graduate level in the Indian medical colleges and Institutions. It is also important to initiate and implement a lesson on how and when to break the bad news as a recognized and innovative model of care. In doing so, it will lead to quality outcomes and will uplift the standard of end-of-life care in India into its new horizon. It will also help in preparing the upcoming physicians and other care providers to be able to equip with proper knowledge, skills, and attitude to communicate effectively and break the bad news without hurting the emotional sentiments of the patient and the loved one. This will also help in creating an environment where one can deliver quality end-of-life care.[11]

The time of breaking bad news is the most crucial moment the patient and family should have ever gone through in their terminally ill experience, and the clinician's responsibility is to help all those involved get through this critical moment in the most effective ways. It is the true information with effective communication skills that serves as the key element in dealing with the breaking of bad news in any clinical practice. Unlike the other news, it is the news that destroys the peaceful mind as it contains stress, anxiety, and discomfort the task of delivering becomes more difficult for clinicians working in end-of-life care. The interventions of the multi-disciplinary team that can address the patient and family, psychological issues, emotional sufferings, and mental disharmony alongside the deliverance of the bad news can encounter this crucial moment in the appropriate ways in the clinical setting, which would even help in the bereavement policy. The inclusion of delivering the bad news in clinical practice in the training of medical professionals in their undergraduate program is the underlying challenge in the present situation. The absence of delivering the bad news in the medical curriculum resulted in clinicians dealing with the breaking of the bad news in the most unsuccessful ways. Carrying out research work on how to manage the patient and family's psycho-emotional challenges and mental needs in and after the breaking of the bad news is the urgent need of the hour. On the other hand, the involvement of well-trained psychologists in clinical practices could solve most of the underlying issues around the breaking of the bad news in end-of-life care.

Reference

1. Gregg K Vandekieft. Breaking Bad News. Am Fam Physician, 2001; 15;64(12):1975-1979. https://www.aafp.org/afp/2001/1215/p1975.pdf.

2. Vijayakumar Narayanan, Bibek Bista and Cheriyan Koshy. BREAKS' Protocol for Breaking Bad News. Indian J Palliat Care. 2010; 16(2): 61–65. Doi: 10.4103/0973-1075.68401.

3. Buckman R. How to Break Bad News: A Guide for Health Care Professionals. Baltimore: Johns Hopkin University Press, 1992.

4. Buckman R. Make Bad News Easier Conversations in Care, 2007. conversationsincare.com/web_book/chapter05.html. Accessed on November 27, 2019.

5. Hawryluck Laura. Ian Anderson Continuing Education Program in End-of-Life Care, Module 5: Communication With Patients and Families. Toronto: University of Toronto, 2000.

6. Rajashree C. Communication Skill. Certificate Courses in Essentials of Palliative Care. Lucknow: Indian Association of Palliative Care, 2011.

7. Irish Hospice Foundation. How Do I Break Bad News, 2013. hospicefoundation.ie/2013/04/how-do-break-bad-news. Pdf. Accessed on November 27, 2019.

8. African Palliative Care Association. Palliative Care: A Handbook of Palliative Care in Africa. Kampala: African Palliative Care Association, 2010.

9. Rosenzweig MQ. Breaking bad news: A Guide For Effective And Empathetic Communication. Nurse Pract. 2012 Feb 12; 37(2): 1–4. Doi: 10.1097/01.NPR. 0000408626.24599.9e.

10. Walter F. Bailea, Robert Buckmanb, Renato Lenzia, Gary Globera, Estela A. Bealea and Andrzej P. Kudelkab. SPIKES—A Six-Step Protocol for Delivering Bad News: Application to the Patient with Cancer. http://theoncologist.alphamedpress.org /content/5/4/302.long. Accessed on November 29, 2019.

11. Suantak Demkhosei Vaiphei, Devendra Sisodia Singh. The emerging needs of effective communication in palliative end-of-life care: a qualitative review. J Clin Med Kaz. 2019; 3(53):11-15.

CHAPTER – NINE

Existential Therapeutic Intervention and Positive Health Outcomes

Abstract

There is no easy way to deliver a quality of life in caring for the distressing physical pain, discomfort, and psychological symptoms like emotional suffering and mental disharmony in the clinical settings; it requires maximum amounts of effort and attention attained by the multidisciplinary teams, which is just a myth in the context of Indian palliative end-of-life care at present. Psychotherapeutics is essential to critical care medicine in terminal diagnosis, it helps the patient discover one's meaning and purpose in suffering which gives the dying patient a sense of hope to recreate and reframe the goals of life in his/her terminally ill experience. The interventions of the psychological approach in terminal care will give awareness to the terminally ill patients that he/she is still in the conditions of the limitless possibilities of achievements in their life.

Key Words: Existential Therapy, Intervention, Psychotherapy, Critical care, and Psychological Approach

Introduction

End-of-life care is an interdisciplinary program mainly focusing on people suffering from various terminal illnesses, who are at the stage of their limited prognosis. At present the upcoming advances in medical technology, diagnostics and other antibiotic therapies, and critical care have created bioethical dilemmas that confront physicians while dealing with patients who are at their end of life. This tends to aggravate the isolation and loneliness experienced by the dying patients. Existential and spiritual suffering at the end of life are the most debilitating conditions, yet the most neglected area of care. [1,2] Existential therapy, on the other hand, though the most neglected area of care, addresses issues that preoccupy many terminally ill patients from alienation and loneliness to depersonalization, and most importantly with meaning. Existential psychotherapy more than any other existing therapies, provides a set of fundamental principles that serve as guidelines and structures for meaning-making in end-of-life care.[2] Dying patient as a human needs holistic care, which could treat him/her with dignity, rather than being used as an experimental object or as a laboratory for modern medicines.

Existential psychotherapy is not just a philosophy, rather, a critical care medicine that treats humans by providing hope when a cure is not possible. It is a therapy, which transforms the dying patient by providing purpose, peace, and meaningful death, and dying. Psychotherapy acknowledges the meaning and purpose in life as an important instrument for quality of life and helps the dying individual to look at the human condition as a whole and their place within it. The focus of existential psychotherapy is to form a balance between being aware of death without being overwhelmed by death, which will lead to quality decision-making in the face of death and dying. However, the challenges are, how then shall we apply and implement existential therapy in the clinical setting?

Psychotherapeutic Intervention in End-of-Life Assessment

"End-of-life care is an interdisciplinary medical specialty that focuses on preventing and relieving suffering and on supporting the best quality of life (QOL) for patients who are facing a serious or life-threatening illness and their families." [3] End-of-life care is a care that helps all those with advanced, progressive, incurable illnesses to live as well as possible until they die. The key issues in end-of-life care include pain and symptom control, shared decision-making, psychological and spiritual support, and alternative sites of care. A maximum amount of care and attention needs to be provided to distressing pain and non-pain symptoms including physical discomfort, emotional suffering, and functional limitations affecting quality of life.[4] However, in most clinical settings, clinicians frequently underestimate the potential benefits of psychotherapy for seriously medically ill patients, especially for those patients who are months far from death, when the psychotherapeutic approaches have been proven to be effective for patients struggling with advanced, life-threatening medical illness. There is a psychological dimension to the work of all involved in palliative care and understanding this will strengthen the practice of any professional working in the end-of-life care area. In special palliative care contexts, the generic skills of the psychologist are applied in a setting where a person has either been given a terminal diagnosis, is a relative or close friend of such a person, or has been bereaved because of the death of such a person. Primary care psychologists are in a prime position to help patients, their families, and other health care professionals to navigate and coordinate care along the disease continuum and maximize quality of life no matter the patient's prognosis.[2,5] The impact of terminal illness on one's life can be related to four factors: The Existential threat of the disease, psychological consequences, Consequences of the morbid disease process, and the Treatment and its effect. Psychotherapy plays an important role as it supports having a better chance to be able to release built-up tension and anxiety.[6] The four important keys for psychological assessment in end-of-life care are: [7,8]

- Psychologists are already extensively involved in the treatment of the chronic illness such as heart disease and cancer which are now the leading causes of death and health care expenditure.
- Chronic illness imposes extensive coping demands on patients and families, and psychologists contribute significantly to the treatment of the major disorders of our time: heart disease, cancer, AIDS, dementia, diabetes, chronic pain and respiratory ailments, and multiple sclerosis, among others.
- The active role of psychologists in the treatment of chronic and life-threatening conditions has been supported by a second key development: the emergence of the biopsychosocial model in medicine and clinical health psychology.
- The evolution of psychological practice in end-of-life care is also being shaped by their development: a broad-based effort currently underway to improve life's final passage for patients and loved ones.

Psychologists have a potentially central role in end-of-life care as they are trained to help others explore and make sense of their hopes, aspirations, achievements, disappointments, and relationships. Most specifically, they can provide expert intervention where needed. The psychotherapeutic relationship gives the patient a feeling of comfort and certainty of being respected and valued which helps them view life differently apart from being ill. The underlying existential questions are: how can we meet the patient's needs so that they can die at home and avoid treatments that violate their preferences? How can we, as health care providers and as a society, guarantee people a peaceful, meaningful death?[9] There are no easy answers, but spirituality is a very important part of the solution. Good palliative care practice obliges us to acknowledge the innate existential nature of distress that accompanies the experience of dying people. Researchers recognizing the importance of existential or spiritual issues for dying patients have begun to conceptually parse out and examine the effect of hopelessness, burden to others, loss of sense of dignity, and loss of will to live on patients approaching death.[10] Palliative care informed by spiritual attentiveness allows both the patient and the provider to give up illusions of therapeutic entitlement to cure and at the same time honor the privilege of intentional and reverent caring for the dying. The suggested approaches to be addressed in the treatment of the dying include Controlling Physical Symptoms; Providing a Supportive Presence; Encouraging Life Review to Help Recognize Purpose, Value, and Meaning; Exploring Guilt, Remorse, Forgiveness, and Reconciliation; Facilitating Religious Expression; Reframing Goals; and Encouraging Meditative Practices Focused on Healing Rather than on Cure.[11] Spirituality in terminal illness focuses on increasing patients' sense of meaning and purpose in life. This meaning-centered approach is deeply rooted in existential theory and therapeutic practice.

Existential Psychotherapy and the Search for Meaning

Existential psychotherapy is a philosophical method of therapy that operates on the belief that inner conflict within a person is due to the individual's confrontation with the "givens" of existence. The givens are the inevitability of death, freedom and its attendant responsibility, existential isolation, and meaninglessness. Existential psychotherapy is based upon the principles of psychodynamic therapy, humanistic, and existential psychology and is often misperceived as some morbid, arcane, pessimistic, impractical, cerebral, esoteric treatment.[12] However, the truth is an exceedingly practical, concrete, positive, and flexible approach. Existential psychology has also been influenced by artistic expressions of the confusion and alienation that people experience in their confrontation with meaningless and absurdity, which are found during the mid-twentieth century in the work of novelists like Dostoevsky and Kafka, and existentialist writers Sartre, de Bouvoir, Camus, Ionesco, and Beckett.[13] Yalom was the first to complete a manual on existential psychotherapy which delivered both theoretical structure and practical techniques for an approach. Yalom explains existential psychotherapy as a dynamic therapeutic approach that focuses on concerns rooted in existence and asserts that holding an awareness of these issues can profoundly influence the nature of the therapist-client relationship. In end-of-life care, patients are frequently confronted with several existential symptoms and spiritual distress that challenge the palliative care providers. though existential and spiritual suffering are among the most debilitating conditions in dying patients but are neglected areas of care because of the confusion over definition, lack of conceptual understanding, few documented interventions, and the absence of appropriate training among the palliative care providers. Existential psychotherapy is a type of therapy that emphasizes the human condition by using a positive approach that appreciates human capacities and aspirations while simultaneously acknowledging human limitations. It is based upon the fundamental belief that all people experience intrapsychic conflict due to their interaction with certain conditions inherent in human existence such as Freedom and associated responsibility; Death; Isolation; and Meaningless. [14]

Existential psychotherapy strives to empower and place the person and his or her existential choices back at the center of the therapeutic process. Choice, personal, and social responsibility, integrity of the personality, courage, and authentically facing rather than escaping existential anxiety, anger, and guilt are central features of existential psychotherapy. The emerging interest in existential suffering follows several themes which include definitional understandings, the needs of patients, interventions, theories of existential suffering, methods and designs, and responses of palliative providers who care for patients at the end of life. Existential psychotherapy explores what it means to be human in the light of our shared human condition; that is, we may live in infinite possibilities, but we are essentially finite creatures. [15,16] The following six propositions underlie the basis of existential psychotherapy that can serve as guidelines while working with dying patients: [17,18]

- The capacity for self-awareness (we are finite, yet we have the potential to continually grow and become until we die)
- Freedom and responsibility (we can commit to authentically choose a life for ourselves)
- The need for center and the need for others (we can have the courage to be, as well as the experience of aloneness and relatedness)
- The search for meaning (we can discard old values, freely choose new ones, and continually question and challenge the meaning of life)

- Anxiety as a condition of living (we can experience anxiety as a source of growth, and we can experience the escape from anxiety)
- Awareness of death and nonbeing (the very realization of eventual nonbeing gives meaning to existence because it makes every human act count).

The existential therapist is not confined to the passive, neutral, anonymous, and interpretive role of the psychoanalyst. The existential therapist requires the courage and commitment to encounter each unique patient truly and genuinely and must not avoid his/her anxiety by hiding behind a rigid professional persona or route therapeutic technique. Existential psychotherapy doesn't only address emotional issues but also teaches people in therapy to grow and embrace their own lives and exist in them with wonder and curiosity. This therapy does not focus on a person's past, rather, works with the person in therapy to discover and explore the choices that lie in them. Through this work, people often come to feel both a sense of liberation and the ability to let go of the despair associated with insignificance and meaninglessness. However, the value of existential psychotherapy in end-of-life care is that it encourages patients to seriously explore their past, present, and future in terms of meaningful choices and the experiences that created and continue to generate their stories. Breitbart and colleagues also stated that existential therapists offer dying patients a way to bear the burden of their suffering and eventual death with strength and dignity by helping patients explore the "why" of their existence and the meaning of their lives.[19] Patients meaningfully reflect upon and take ownership of the lives they have chosen and of the possibilities that are still available until the moment of their death.

Significance of Existential Psychotherapy

Existential therapy guides the clients in learning to take responsibility for their own choices and making choices that align with their values and help them to live more authentically. It is not necessarily to learn certain skills or pick up a particular habit, but rather to form a realistic and authentic relationship with life. Existential therapists have the advantage of hindsight. It proceeds through the relationship and the psychotherapist functions as guide, accompanist, and symbol. The therapist has confronted the givens of existence and significantly worked through existential anxiety toward more effective integration. In existential therapy, the human relationship between patient and therapist takes precedence over technical tricks, and as now corroborated by research, is the basic healing factor in any psychotherapy.[20] The real comfort can come only in the relationship of the therapist and the client or patient. In focusing upon the various inter-relational realms, existential psychotherapy, through their acts of collaborative and clarifying dialogue can provide the potential for transformative experience. This compassionate, shared, professional yet profoundly personal human relationship provides both the structured, supportive container and potent existential catalyst for therapeutic transformations. Existential psychotherapy is the only established form of psychotherapy that is directly based on philosophy rather than psychology. It focuses on the intra-personal dimensions of human existence and has formulated psychological theories that do not allow the philosophical dimension to come to the fore or to be central. The issue of how to address patients' existential needs may be linked to how well the phenomenon of existential suffering is understood or whether it is viewed as a concept distinct from that of spirituality.[21] However, the concepts of spiritual and existential suffering are neither discussed separately nor acknowledged as having different meanings.

The central claim of existentialism is that existence precedes essence. The significance lies in addressing issues that preoccupy so many people, from alienation and loneliness to depersonalization, and above all, it offers meaning. It stresses the value and importance of individual experience, and one is not defined by his/her past and is free to create his/her own life and identity and must take responsibility for this. Radical existential psychotherapy focuses on the inter-personal and supra-personal dimensions, as it tries to capture and question people's worldviews. They aim at clarifying and understanding personal values and beliefs and seek to enable a person to live more deliberately, more authentically, and more purposefully while accepting the limitations and contradictions of human existence. An existential psychotherapist is symbolized as the wounded healer who recognizes both aspects of the wounded/healing polarity as existing within oneself. The psychotherapist apprehends these things with humility and in helping the patient, it also heals himself or herself. Some existential thinkers like Binswanger (1963), Yalom (1980), and Deurzen (1984), avoid restrictive models that categorize or label people, rather look for the universal hypothesis that can be observed cross-culturally. To them, there is no existential personality theory that divides humanity into types or reduces people to different components.[20] There is a description of the different levels of experience and existence with which people are inevitably confronted. They stated that how a person is in the world at a particular stage can be charted on this general map of human existence.

Meaning and Anxiety in Existential Psychotherapy

It is important to note another view of existential psychotherapy, that life has meaning under all circumstances. Victor Frankl's, as one of the basic tenets in his logotherapy includes that life has meaning under all circumstances, even under suffering. Meaninglessness then is meaning not yet discovered. Existentialism has a unique perspective on meaning that sets it apart from the mainstream philosophies that preceded it that there is no meaning. This is not to say that there is no meaning at all, just that there is no inherent, built-in, or "default" in our world. Whatever meaning is derived from our world is given to it by the individual. If existential therapists prioritize one thing, it would be the search for meaning and the need to feel that your life has meaning. The fundamental question in life states why is there something rather than nothing? The clients ask themselves this question regularly and they are unclear about the meaning of their own life. Such a question is necessary to become a self-reflective human being. Existentialism is based on the fundamental premise that human beings have the unique capacity to question and reflect upon their existence. Doubt and wonder enable humans to discover the miracle of being. The existential aim is to liberate patients from being passive victims of circumstance and invite them to become active participants in their lives through heightened awareness and responsibility. [8,20] Taking meaningful ownership of one's life, feelings, choices, and beliefs promotes authentic relatedness with oneself, the world, and others. It is not an easy task to be truly available to help others find meaning in their lives when their existence is in crisis. The meaning of life is never given and cannot be transmitted unless a person is willing to search for it independently. Inner peace develops from finding clarity on what we want life to be about and understanding what truly matters to us as an individual, outside of the influence of others and even society. [5,7]

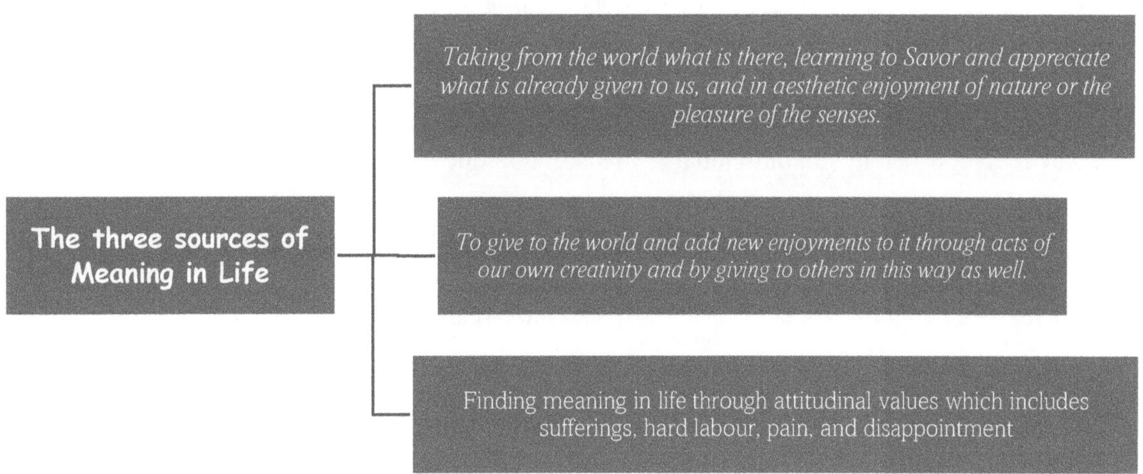

According to existential thought, we must look within ourselves to find meaning, assert our values, and to make the decisions that shape our lives. Existential therapy is an excellent method for threatening the psychological and emotional instabilities or dysfunctions that stem from the basic anxieties of human life. Yalom proposes that human beings should confront death anxiety in the same way they confront any fear. Existentialism proposes that it is possible in one's life to face anxieties head-on and embrace the human condition of loneliness, to revel in the freedom to choose and take full responsibility for their choices. one does not need to arrest feelings of meaninglessness, but can choose new meanings for their lives, and be able to live life as one's adventure. [9,10] For existential psychotherapists the experience of anxiety is the fundamental 'given' of being in the world. The responses that individuals raise to minimize, deny, or repress intolerable levels of anxiety are, in themselves, central factors in subsequent experiences of sedimentation and dissociation, confusion, learned helplessness, and denial of freedom. Human suffering as an individual experience is a central theme in the thinking and writing of existentialists. One must become an independent force and an individual, which demands the ability to be alone and to reflect quietly within us and an inmate knowledge of our suffering. The experience of meaninglessness and the creation of meaning is closely related to the experience of Angst or existential anxiety. It occurs against the backdrop of the personal realization of aloneness, a sense of mortality, and other limitations, taking responsibility for oneself in the face of endless challenges and confusion. Victor Frankl in his study of "Man search for meaning," pointed out that, what is important is not an action in and of itself, but the way action is experienced, the intensity with which life is lived, and the notion that a person can choose freely his or her response to a given situation.[12] What makes a person is not determined by type, but by who he/she becomes, and it is within this understanding that facticity, transcendence, alienation, and authenticity must be understood. Anxiety or Angst is a core concept in existential philosophy, which sees it as the basic ingredient of vitality. Learning to be anxious in the right way is the key to living a reflective and meaningful life. In the words, existential therapy, unlike other therapeutic approaches, argues that "the source of conflict in an individual's life are not due to instinctual demands that are not being sufficiently met or that are in conflict with opposing demands, nor are they directly due to conflicts with significant others, or misunderstood, incomplete or improper learning experiences, but, rather, they lie with the ontological 'givens' of human inter-relational existence such as temporality, freedom, encounter, and meaning/meaninglessness, and the degree to which each individual responds to these either to minimize or to deny the anxiety they provoke via the construction and adoption of his/her worldview."[9,11]

Thus, the principles of existential therapy extend to a widening clinical domain, and its perspectives apply far beyond the clinical setting. The principles of freedom, experiential reflection, and responsibility are being propagated in work and educational settings and even in religious and political realms as well. The psychotherapeutic process of existential therapy is then to elicit, clarify, and put into perspective all the current issues and contradictions that are problematic. The ultimate therapeutic search is about allowing the client to reclaim personal freedom and a willingness and ability to be open to the world in all its complexity. [12] Though existential issues in the end-of-life care context have remained widely used, it is sad to say that it is yet an ill-defined concept, a neglected symptom of suffering, and little is known about its effectiveness concerning interventions. It is high time to systematically explore existential psychotherapeutic intervention by removing the confusion in the palliative care context, as its goal is to use coping most effectively by enhancing patients' sense of meaning and purpose. Meaning-centered psychotherapy is an existential attempt to explore the complex relationship between meaning and illness. It also offers a therapeutic and healing alternative that may help patients confront the existential challenges presented by life-threatening illness. [13] Within the existential psychotherapeutic relationship, the therapist is the other who serves as a representative of all others in the client's wider world relations. Most importantly, the therapist is also the other who challenges the client's beliefs and assumptions regarding others and their impact on his or her way of being. Perhaps, the lack of conceptual understanding also resulted in the confusion of its implementation in clinical settings. The existing literature points to the importance of sensitivity and trust relations, as well as to an awareness of the individual nature of patients' existential concerns. The challenges of assessing and treating the existential domains include consideration of the subjective nature of its expression and the personal experiences of vulnerability by clinicians who witness their patients' suffering. Existential psychotherapy can indeed take many different shapes and forms, but it always requires a philosophical exploration of what is true for the patient [7,10]. Authentic living with courage and humility would be a suitable existential objective, and another objective would be learning to reflect on oneself and effectively communicating with others. Effective implementation of existential psychotherapy in palliative care can contribute to desperately needed reform that exchanges the palliatives and absolutisms so prevalent in the world for complexity, discernment, and inquiry. This is a reform by which all healers are being summoned and challenged. [15,16]

Further Challenges and Conclusion

Existential psychotherapy begins where the existing medical system and formula end, by dealing with four dimensions of approach to end-of-life care, such as Physical, Social, Psychological, and Spiritual dimension. However, as per the findings of this review, there has been a lack of consistency in the way existential psychotherapy is defined and understood mostly in Indian clinical settings. However, it is important for clinicians and other care providers working in the end-of-life care environment to be mindful of their own choices and consider treatment options from a critical approach. [1,2] Existential psychotherapy is a revolutionary therapy that seeks to find ways to improve well-being, and the patient's version of purpose and meaning in suffering and dying, which modern medicine fails to provide. Existential therapy also encounters the medical realms and world on different levels that connect to give the dying patient its definition of reality, freedom of choice, and to overcome anxieties about life under any circumstances. It seeks to give positive changes in one's life and help them to move forward with a life that the dying individual wants to live, and a better future within a limited time- period for the survivor. Most importantly, it seeks purpose and meaning and the need to feel that one's life has its unique meaning, which every human is longing to have. The therapy also helps to develop awareness of the principles and theories that are given before or during participating in the treatment.

Existential therapy, which is quite adaptable in clinical settings, is often used along with other approaches to terminally ill-treatment. Combining both medical and existential approaches in end-of-life care can maximize the effectiveness of both and promote a greater sense of recovery. Even the worldview of the dying patient towards self, illness, and others will also be enlarged, resulting in a better quality of life in the face of death and dying.

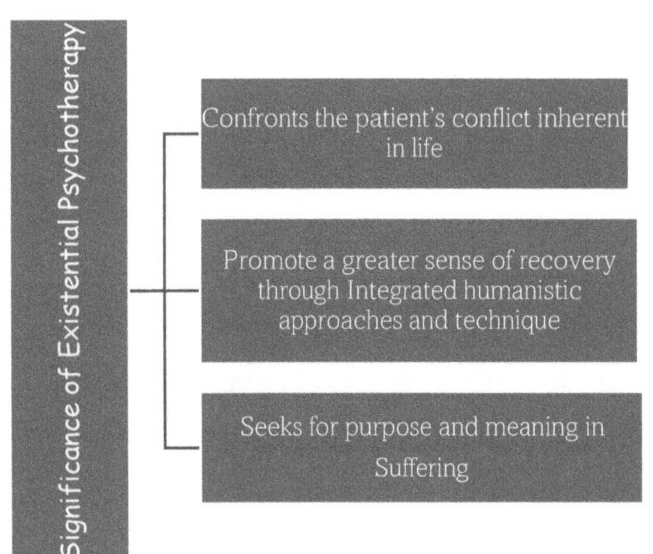

Existential psychotherapy has produced some of the most eloquent case studies in the professional literature and helps terminally ill patients in many ways in the course of their illness, which is mostly characterized by physical pain and emotional suffering. At the same time, it is also important to know its limitations in the clinical setting. On the other hand, though existential psychotherapy can take many shapes and forms in its approach, it always requires a philosophical exploration of what is true for the client and leads to greater recognition of what is true for human beings in general, affording the beginning of a genuinely philosophical stance, which may make it easier to tackle life's inevitable darkness and adversity. In general, though existential psychotherapy may incorporate techniques or ideas from other forms of therapy, such as cognitive, behavioral, narrative, and others, all existential therapy sessions depend on the productive and close relationship between therapist and client to succeed. [17,18]

It can provide an awareness of one's inner resources during the existing sufferings and challenges. It often seeks a way out to make the impossible possible and sometimes succeeds in many ways by providing constant joy, delight, a celebration of life, perfect love, and freedom. Even though providing a setting in which one enhances self-consciousness as one comes to see things more nearly as they are and, increasingly, experience one's existence as real, however, when it comes to the long run, existential psychotherapy has its limitations in providing the characteristics for meaningful and happy life in coexisting with the world and illness. The challenges lie in how patients experience existential suffering, the various assessments for existential concerns in clinical settings, and the process of delivering existential psychotherapy to patients and families. There is also an emerging need for end-of-life care provider's self-reflective responses to existential suffering. The quality of life and person-centered care/therapy can be achieved through the humanity approach and sharing the concern for those wishes shared by the dying individuals. There is an emerging need to modify this psychotherapeutic model and practice in all its forms, as we are living in a changing world, so does the psychotherapeutic approach also need to evolve to meet human needs.

References

1. Achenbach, B.G. *Philosophische Praxis*. Koln/Cologne: Jurgen Dinter, 1984.

2. Ackerman, Courtney. Existential Therapy: Make Your Own Meaning. *Positivepsychologyprogram.com/existential-therapy*. Retrieved from the web 12 February 2022.

3. Banalities. What is Existential Psychotherapy?. *www.harleytherapy.co.uk/counselling/what-is-existential-psychotherapy.html*. Retrieved from the web 14 March 2022.

4. Binswanger, L. Being-in-the-World, Transl. Needleman J. New York: Basic Books, 1967.

5. Boston, Patricia et al. Existential Suffering in the Palliative Care Setting: An Integrated Literature Review. *Journal of pain and Symptom Management*. 2011; 41 (3): 604-618..

6. Breitbart, William. Et al. Psychotherapeutic Interventions at End of Life: A Focus on Meaning and Spirituality. *Can J Psychiatry*. 2004; 49 (6): 366-372.

7. Chochinov, Max Harvey. Dying, Dignity, and New Horizons in Palliative End-of-Life Care. *A Cancer Journal for Clinicians*. 2006; 56 (2): 84-100.

8. Deurzen, Emmy Van. Existentialism and Existential Psychotherapy. *Researchgate.net/publication/265245397_ existentialism and existential psychotherapy*. Retrieved from the web 14 March 2022.

9. Deurzen-Smith, E. Van. *Existential Counseling in Practice*. London: Sage Publications, 1998.

10. Deurzen-Smith, E. Van. *Everyday Mysteries: Existential Dimensions of Psychotherapy*. London: Routledge, 1997.

11. Deurzen, Emmy Van. Existentialism and Existential Psychotherapy. *www.researchgate.net/publication/265245397_existentialismandexistential_psychotherapy*. Retrieved from the web November 2023.

12. Frank, V.E. *Man's Serach For Meaning*. London: Hooder and Stoughton, 1946.

13. Frankl, VE. *Man's Search For Meaning*. New York: Plenum Press, 1997.

14. Breitbart, William. Et al. Psychotherapeutic Interventions at End of Life: A Focus on Meaning and Spirituality. *Can J Psychiatry*, 2014; 49 (6): 366-372.

15. Haley, E. William. Et al. Roles of Psychologists in End-of-Life Care: Emerging Models of Practice. *Professional Psychology: Research and Practice*. 2003; 34 (6 626-633.

16. Kasl-Godley, Julia E et al. Opportunities for Psychologists in Palliative care. *American psychologist*. 2014; 69 (4): 364-376.

17. Yalom, I. *Existential Psychotherapy*. New York: Basic Books, 1980.

18. Yalom, I.D. *Staring at the sun*. San Francisco: Jossey-Bass, 2008.

CHAPTER – TEN

The Art of Spiritual-Psychotherapeutic Model of Care

Abstract

There is no doubt that modern scientific medicine helps in sustaining human life but tends to forget terminal ill experiences are unlike other illnesses accompanied by several mental and psychological factors. This imbalance or disharmony of body, mind, and spirit demands special needs assessment. Alongside the empirical evidence, there is a consensus in the literature about the influence of spirituality on recovery and the ability to cope with and adjust to the even when a cure is not possible. Spiritual psychotherapy is a modern humanistic approach with a holistic view of human illness in health and medical sciences. It serves as an effective coping mechanism to cope and deliver quality of life through its meaning-making policy in clinical settings. The present study is based on empirical work on spirituality and culture to develop a discourse on palliative care and spirituality. Though challenging, responding to spiritual needs could reward the patient, family, and clinicians. It could serve as the source for improving quality of life, resolutions, meaning, and purpose in life. The author does propose that spiritual assessment could also derive great health benefits for those patients with terminal ill diagnoses.

Key Words: Spiritual Assessment, End-of-Life care, Depression; Anxiety, Well-Being, terminally ill, and Dying Individuals.

Introduction

With the rapidly increasing cancer mortality rates, India stood as the main contributor across the continent. The rapidly growing terminally ill population makes quality end-of-life care more important than the process of prolonging the patient's life in clinical settings. Among all the existing models of care, palliative end-of-life care acknowledges the significance of spirituality in assessing the needs of patients and their families. Yet, psycho-spiritual issues are found to be the most underrepresented in Indian clinical practices and research on palliative care. The psycho-spiritual dimension has less of a representation than physical symptom management. In the human experience, spirituality is understood as the core element of health, illness, and dying. This makes spiritual assessment an essential component in palliative end-of-life care, and it is the responsibility of the clinicians and other caregivers to explore the spiritual needs of the patients and families. In terminally ill experience, spirituality can encompass the patient's search for meaning and purpose, also the connections the individual makes with others, and themselves outside the existing traditional religion.[1]

In a clinical setting, spirituality is re-defined in terms of the love and care relationship towards the terminally ill patient, not only confined to a sense of relatedness to the higher transcendent being.[2] With the upcoming advances in medical technology, diagnostics, and other antibiotic therapies, critical care has created bioethical dilemmas that confront physicians while dealing with terminally ill patients who are at their end of life. Moreover, physicians are less trained in providing good end-of-life care, which tends to worsen the condition of isolation and loneliness experienced by dying patients.[3] Palliative end-of-life care is an interdisciplinary program of care for people suffering from terminally ill conditions and those having a limited prognosis. The modern hospice defines the unit of care as the care that provides the patient's care in the context of his or her family or care unit. The hospices on the other hand help the family deal effectively with issues associated with the dying and death of a family member. Hospice is a holistic and philosophical approach to end-of-life care, and it is care given to a person when there is no hope for living. [4,5] End-of-life care offers specialization to those who are suffering from terminal illnesses. The primary goal is to provide comfort and care for those with life-limiting illness and their families so that the patients might be able to die peacefully in the setting of their choice while receiving all necessary nursing, medical, psychological, and spiritual care.

The Interface Between Psychology and Spirituality in End-of-Life Care

Most people assume that religion and spirituality as interchangeable terms in their nature of existence. But when it comes to the palliative care setting, they are different from one another and it's important to identify their differences, as spirituality is not confined within the existing religions or the belief systems. The fundamental principle of effective spiritual care lies in recognizing the fact that spirituality has a broader concept than that of religious concerns. Religion can be seen as the corporate, bounded within its doctrinal realms, and organized outward expression of a belief system. However, the spiritual dimension is common to everyone with its primary aim being to search for meaning in every situation of life.[6,7] Unlike religious belief, spirituality is a factor that covers several meanings, with religious or non-religious beliefs, whereas, religion is a specific set of beliefs and practices related to faith, which recognize, approach, and facilitate access to the sacred, the divine, God, and absolute truth. It is mainly based on a set of scriptures and doctrinal teachings that generally offer a moral code of conduct. Spirituality is a process or a journey of self-discovery and self-learning for not only who you are, but also who you want to become. Spirituality is a dynamic, evolving process, one that impacts and is impacted by an individual's life experience.[8]

Religion, on the other hand, is an organized system of beliefs, practices, and symbols that are characteristic to make more possible ways to be closer to God. It is the search for significance that is related to the sacred, which encompasses both the personal and social, traditional, and non-traditional forms of the religious search activities. To assess health-relevant domains of religiousness and spirituality for use in health outcomes research includes: [5,9]

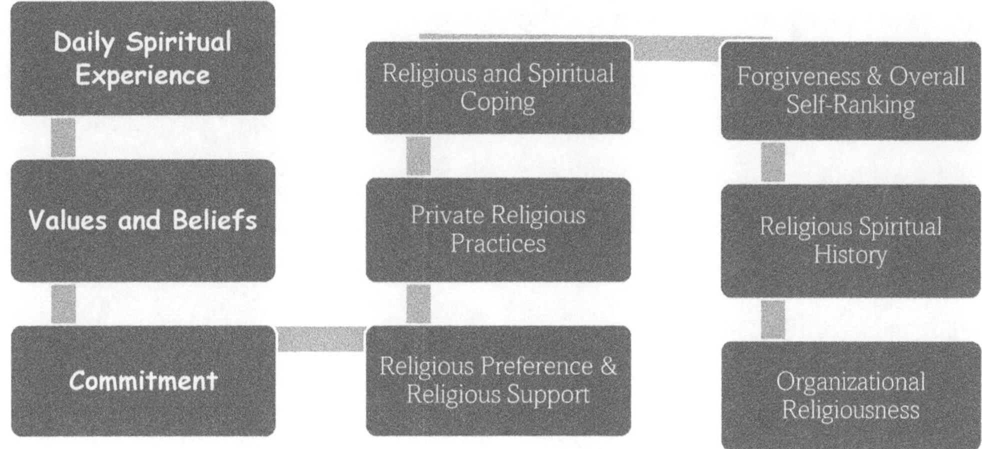

Spirituality may or may not be connected to religious beliefs and practices, but as terminally ill patients acknowledge a greater perspective of spirituality than those non-terminally ill, the psychological states and quality-of-life outcomes have been the primary focus in end-of-life care studies.[9] A person is intrinsically spiritual as in a true relationship with the transcendent being, and sickness is understood as a disruption of that right relationship. So, the appropriate care of the dying person requires attention to the restoration of all the interpersonal and extra-personal relationships that can still be addressed.[10] It is evident that the successful application of the concepts about spirituality in clinical settings and practice is directly connected to the construction of knowledge underlying the assistance, and can be accomplished through the development of new research and skills for healthcare approaches in the various scenarios of professional practice.

Spirituality and Meaning-Making in End-of-Life Care

Human illness is a mixture of biomedical and molecular biology, which requires the need to focus on the whole person's treatment that includes the physical, psychological, and social, dimensions. The biological assessment deals with an understanding of the causes of the illness from the biological factors, and the psychological assessment deals with the psychological factors like self-control, mental disorder, and negative outcomes of the illness. The social assessment investigates how social factors like the socioeconomic status of the patient and culture can influence patients' terminally ill experiences. The spiritual domain on the other hand focuses on the individual relationship with the transcendent influencing the individual health conditions. [3,5] The modern era terminal ill diagnosis should deliver holistic assessment as humans are in a relationship with their biological factors and the transcendent being. The spiritual psychotherapeutic approach to illness addresses the patient's total existence the physical, psychological, social, and spiritual domains are considered. It serves as a patient-centered therapy that acknowledges the whole person's treatment in any terminal assessment and makes them understand their illness. [4,9] Victor Frank [5] stated in any ill experience humans are not destroyed by the suffering in the illness, rather they are destroyed by suffering without meaning in it. Thus, the process of meaning-making in terminal illness becomes an important domain of care. The World Health Organization also acknowledges spirituality as an important factor in the quality of life and is considered the tenet of palliative end-of-life care. Spirituality can be defined as a sense of interconnectedness with the transcendent being regarding the purpose, meaning, and absolute values that life bears. Amid helplessness condition spirituality serves as how the individual finds meaning in life, hope, and inner peace in the face of inevitable death.[11]

In developed countries, spirituality is a topic that drives people's interest in health, well-being, and palliative end-of-life care. It is the concept of the dying individual that there is a transcendent dimension that constructs a sense of hope for meaning and purpose in life in the face of medical helplessness. It is through the hope that exists in the individual belief the terminal patient finds peace, which is an integral component in coping with death and dying. Spiritual psychotherapeutic interventions can attend to and satisfy the core needs of the patients.[12] Even clinicians attending to the spiritual needs of dying patients can experience inner peace, besides the effective deliverance of quality of life to the patient and family. Relaying in the transcendent being and prayer play an important role in alleviating pain symptoms and promoting good health in the clinical setting. Spirituality is the key factor having the potential to enhance patient subjective well-being through promoting healthy personal living. It provides meaning in suffering and ensures social support in the community.[13] In wider understanding spirituality is the one mechanism that serves as a source of strength, comfort, and hope. It also helps in decreasing disease risk and enhances health and well-being. Spiritual psychotherapy is a platform to fulfill the dying patient's wishes before the inevitable death strikes. It is the only mechanism that delivers peaceful death and makes dying as normal as death in terminal experiences.[14]

Spirituality is not only the factor that contributes to the health of many but is also recognized as central to the dying individual. Several findings also acknowledge spirituality as the factor that decreases the fear of death and delivers a sense of control over emotional helplessness. It is a universal belief that a strong sense of spirituality in oneself serves as the structure for effective coping mechanisms and experiencing more connectedness to self, others, and the transcendent being amid painful ill experiences. [15] Generally, in the first two stages of the cancer experience patients usually hope for a cure and the absence of illness from their physical body. However, in the third and the fourth stages where cure becomes completely impossible, the patient shifts from cure to healing through quality times of togetherness with their loved ones. Spiritual psychotherapeutic intervention can deliver general life orientation and personal significance. It serves as a coping mechanism that improves the sense of meaning and purpose in life. Spirituality is the most effective mechanism against mental disharmony and psychological traumas. Spirituality serves as the central component and an important agent that safeguards the patients from end-of-life despair and suffering. [9]

To validate the spiritual statuses that participants attributed to themselves, the study assessed behavioral indicators of religiosity asking them to report the frequency of their attendance to religious services as well as the frequency of their praying on a 5-point scale (0 = never; 1 = only in special occasions; 2 = rarely; 3 = at least once a month; 4 = at least once a week; 5 = every day or almost every day).

Spiritual Participants		Non-Spiritual Participants	
Performing/Attending Religious Services/Activities	Regularly Praying	Performing/Attending Religious Services/Activities	Pray Occasionally
60%	41%	0%	0.5%
Uncertain Between Spiritual & Non-Spiritual			
Performing/Attended Religious Services		Prayed only on Special Occasions.	
15%		12%	

Figure – 2: Religious or Spiritual Status.

Spirituality is the factor that allows patients to discover the deeper meaning of existence amid suffering and self-awareness in both the spiritual and non-spiritual patients. As an effective coping mechanism, it helps the dying individual to adjust to their illness, delivers longer life expectancy, and the ability to deal effectively with the pain symptoms. It is the therapy that decreases the amount of depression and anxiety and is successful in reducing the risk behind substance abuse and suicidal activity. [6] Even for loved ones and family, the spiritual psychotherapeutic intervention also serves as a source of meaning and hope, which is less associated with depressive stress symptoms that ignite self-esteem. Spirituality is an essential element for the person-centered care assessment not only increases the rate of patient's positive emotion but also helps in reducing the emotional disorder through its meaning-making policy. Most importantly, spirituality provides an optimistic worldview to the dying patient in the face of medical helplessness and makes sense of their terminal experience. [15] Spirituality in its broader understanding gives meaning to terminal experiences mainly when mental disharmony, depression, and stress strike in the course of illness. Dying in the modern era should be made as natural as that of human birth; it should be a meaningful experience for those facing death and dying. It should be the time when every dying individual finds meaning in their suffering, and the various dimensional needs of the patients are addressed and fulfilled. [7] However, the absence of whole-person treatment in the Indian health care system failed to address the needs of the dying individual and the wishes unfulfilled. Symptoms like depression, anxiety, and other psychological-related issues are considered symptoms not to be treated in its clinical setting.

Analysis and Discussion

The impact of spirituality on health and well-being can be considered invariant regardless of the individual's religious status. The study found a strong impact of spirituality intended as the human desire for transcendence, introspection, interconnectedness, and the quest for meaning in life. This relationship appears the same regardless of the individual's religious status. The finding shows that 85% of terminally ill patients and families felt the need for physicians to acknowledge and address their spiritual needs. However, less than 10% of the patients and families reported their physicians discussing their spiritual beliefs and related issues. The 90% of terminally ill patients and families agreed that physicians/clinicians acknowledging their spiritual needs would strengthen them in the face of inevitable death. Another 97% of inpatients and outpatients for whom spirituality was not important also wanted their physicians to address their spiritual needs and be sensitive towards their beliefs and values framework. Even 80% of the patients who don't believe in any form of an existing religion, do feel the importance of physicians inquiring about their spiritual insights in case of serious illness. The following table will show the data on how terminally ill patients used spirituality as a coping mechanism and a pathway to recovery.

Mortality	Coping	Recovery
70% of the patients with regular spiritual practices tend to live longer	75% of patients utilize their beliefs in coping with illness, pain, and life stresses. 66% acknowledge prayer as a method of pain management was used more frequently than intravenous pain medication	45%-57% acknowledge spiritual commitment tends to enhance recovery from illness and surgery. And 47% felt spirituality is the power of hope and positive thinking
120 older adults showed that those who have regular spiritual practices were half as likely to have elevated levels of interleukin (IL)-6	80% of patients with spirituality have a more positive outlook and a better quality of life	An average of 35% benefited from receiving a placebo for pain, cough, drug-induced mood change, headaches, seasickness, or the common cold when told that the placebo was a drug for their condition.
70% of religious commitment patients show improvement in stress control by offering better-coping mechanisms, richer social support, and the strength of personal values and worldview.	72% of those spiritually active had less fear of death and less guilt. Another 76% of the patient's family members find companionship and spiritual comfort as the best coping mechanism for the bereavement period.	The study found that 67% felt spiritual practices were beneficial for the treatment of chronic pain, insomnia, anxiety, hostility, depression, premenstrual syndrome, and infertility and were a useful adjunct to treatment for patients with cancer or HIV.

<u>**Figure – 3: Spiritual Coping mechanism**</u>

The term health and well-being are not merely free from any physical illness, rather health includes the criteria like mental, physical, psychological, economic, and most importantly the spiritual domain of an individual concerned. It is increasingly visible that both the clinicians and the terminal patients acknowledge the spiritual domain of health care as an important factor of supportive health care in terminal diagnosis to deliver well-being and quality of life.

Spirituality is the mechanism that deals effectively with treatment issues like pain and symptom control, inappropriate prolongation of death and dying, and a patient's feeling of being burdensome to others and loved ones.[9] in concern the positive impacts of spiritual psychotherapy, Manitoba's Spiritual Health Care Partners[10] stated that; spirituality has an impact on the way the terminal patient understand their illness, recovery, and punishment Versus regrettable suffering; quality decision-making about their treatment policy and; building a quality relationship between the terminal patient and the clinicians that usually produces trust and acceptance. Spirituality becomes the central focus in the face of medical helplessness; it helps in effectively coping with a terminal illness and becomes part of their existence that serves as health to many dying patients. The essences of spirituality have the potential to be in communion with self, with others, nature, and with the transcendent being, which delivers the whole person treatment with regards to self-identity, inner peace, love, reconciliation, inspiration, creativity, hope, and gratitude.[11]

Recent research on spirituality in terminal illness intervention found that patients with a higher level of spirituality have a lower risk of depression and anxiety. Through spirituality, the dying individual can effectively construct meaning and purpose in suffering that facilitates a positive role in patients' coping with their illness. The findings stated that even 45% of people with no religious beliefs also felt the need for spiritual assessment in one way or the other and 94% of the cancer patients want their physicians to deliver the spiritual assessment. In many cases, spirituality is seen as the mechanism that has healing potentiality on individual health, influences patient decision-making, and plays an important role in delaying a patient's physical disability which usually occurs in the latter part of any terminal illness. On the other hand, patients with a lower level of spirituality encountered higher rates of stress and depression in their terminally ill experiences. [8,12,13] The new paradigm of spiritual pain and suffering has the sense of emotional diffusion, which is directly related to meaninglessness, and the underlying factor in that pain lies in failing to meet the needs of the dying individual. So, when individuals approach near-death and dying, they usually experience a sense of hopelessness, a burden to others, and lose a sense of dignity in self which usually leads to a loss of will to live.[10]

Thus, spiritual well-being becomes an important dimension that is positively related to the patient's subjective well-being, source of hope, and purpose in life. It is also associated with positive mood stress and the overall quality of life in terminal experience. The importance of spirituality in palliative end-of-life care lies in focusing on the patient's spiritual despair (alienation, loss of oneself, and dissonance); spiritually related workload (forgiveness, self-exploration, search for meaning and balancing life), and well-being of the whole (connectedness, self-actualization, and living in consonance with self and others).[15] At end-of-life, it is evident that terminally ill patients experience mental disharmony, anger, sadness, guilt feeling, anxiety, hopelessness, and the painful feelings of being separated from their loved ones meaning-making becomes a crucial factor. Spirituality, on the other hand, can successfully deliver the immediate context in which dying individuals can make sense of their lives and cope with their illness through the sense of hope that delivers inner peace amid several existential challenges in end-of-life care.[14]

Conclusion

With a broader understanding of health and medical sciences, spirituality has outburst from its limitation within the socio-religious realm. Alongside the advanced modern medical technologies, both the patient and the clinician recognized spirituality as an important domain of care. In the face of medical helplessness, spirituality serves as a coping mechanism that delivers meaning in suffering and quality end-of-life care. However, the absence of the spiritual domain of care failed in delivering the whole person treatment in terminal diagnosis. Dying with dignity and peaceful death is still an unheard topic of care in Indian palliative end-of-life care, mainly due to the absence of biopsychosocial-spiritual therapeutic interventions in its clinical practices. The need of the hour is to acknowledge the fact that health is an interdisciplinary concept and demands a holistic assessment. Assessing physical pain symptoms alone without acknowledging the psycho-spiritual suffering can't deliver quality of life and well-being. It is a spirituality that helps terminal patients deal effectively with their terminal ill experience and adjust accordingly. To overcome depression, stress, anxiety, and other psychological and mental issues associated with terminal ill experience, spirituality is the core factor in the clinical setting.

References

1. Christina M. Puchalski. Spirituality and the care of patients at the end-of-life: an essential component of care. Omega; 56(1): 33-46, 2007-2008. Doi: 10.2190/om.56.1.d.

2. Borrell-Carrio, Francesc., Suchman, Anthony L., & Epstein, Ronald M. The Biopsychosocial Model 25 Years Later: Principles, Practice, and Scientific Inquiry. Ann Fam Med: Annals of Family Medicine. 2004; 2 (6): 576-582. DOI: 10.1370/afm.245.

3. Sulmasy, P. Daniel. A Biopsychosocial-Spiritual Model for the Care of Patients at the End of Life. The Gerontologist. 2002; 42 (3): 24-33.   Doi: org/10.1093/geront/42.suppl_3.24

4. Puchalski, M. Christina. Spirituality in the Cancer Trajectory. Annals of Oncology. 2012; 23 (3): 49-55. Doi: 10.1093/annonc/mds088.

5. Frankl, Victor. Man's Search for Meaning, 4th Edition. Boston: Beacon Press, 1992.

6. World Health Organization. Cancer Control: Knowledge into Action, World Guide for Effective Programmes. Geneva: World Health Organization, 2007.

7. Leyla, F., & Fatemeh, A. Understanding the Role of Spirituality and Faith in Relation to Life Expectancy and End of Life Experience in Terminally Ill Cancer Patients. Gerontol & Geriatric Stud. 2017; 1 (4): 1-10. DOI: 10.4172/2165-7386.C1.005.

8. Puchalski, M. Christina. Spirituality and End-of-Life Care: A Time for Listening and caring. Journal of Palliative Medicine. 2002; 5 (2): 289-294. DOI: 10.1089/109662102753641287.

9. Daaleman, P. Timothy., & VandeCreek, Larry. Placing Religion and Spirituality in End-of-Life Care. JAMA. 2000; 284 (19): 2514-2517. DOI: 10.1001/jama.284.19.2514.

10. Breitbart, William. Et al. Psychotherapeutic Interventions at End of Life: A Focus on Meaning and Spirituality. Can J Psychiatry. 2004; 49 (6): 366-372. DOI: 10.1177/070674370404900605.

11.   Chao, C.C., Chen, C & Yen, M. The Essence of Spirituality of Terminally Ill Patients. Journal of Nursing Research. 2002; 10 (4): 37-44. DOI: 10.1097/01.jnr.0000347604.89509.bf.

12.   Chochinov, Max Harvey. Dying, Dignity, and New Horizons in Palliative End-of-Life Care. CA A Cancer Journal for Clinicians. 2006; 56 (2): 84-103. Doi.org/10.3322/canjclin.56.2.84

13.   Rego, Francisca., & Nunes, Rui. The Interface Between Psychology and Spirituality in Palliative Care. Journal of Health Psychology. 2016; 24(3):279-287. Doi: 10.1177/ 1359105316664138

14.   Holloway, Margret et al. Spiritual Care at the End of Life: A Systematic Review of Literature. London: University of Hull, 2001.

15.   Nwogu, Abel. Wellbeing in Palliative Care: A Literature Review. https://www.theseus.fi/bitstream/handle/10024/76781/my%20thesis.pdf?sequence =1&isAllowed=y. Accessed on 20th November 2022.

Epilogue

Dealing with cancer is a challenging experience of reorganizing life to be a part of the treatment process. Diagnosed with cancer is a life-changing experience for both patient and family with several negative feelings like shock, disbelief, confusion, anger, despair, hopelessness, and guilt. The severity of a patient's distressing symptoms during and after cancer treatment is the underlying predictor of later adjudgment disorders. Almost all the existing research studies reported adjustment disorder as the most prevalent psychiatric disorder. Adjustment disorder is an acute stress response that usually interferes significantly with daily life functioning. Majority of the cancer patients and survivors have adjustment disorders mainly depressed and anxious moods with mixed emotional disturbances. Mental health is a great concern for those with cancer and their caregivers. It affects emotional, interpersonal, rehabilitative, and psychosocial domains contributing to psychosocial distressing symptoms. The timely psycho-oncological assessment improves the quality of life, decreases cancer risk development, and cancer rehabilitation. However, there are no societal or standard guidelines for psychosocial care in India, due to lack of awareness, and stigma associated with cancer. Identifying the pathway to integrate psycho-oncological services into the existing cancer care in a structured manner could improve the treatment outcomes and provide satisfactory cancer care services.

In developed countries, psycho-oncology is a sub-field within oncology and a well-established field of study in the biomedical world. Currently, India has only three psycho-oncology institutions providing professional degrees - Cancer Institute (WIA), Chennai; Center of Psycho-oncology for Education and Research (COPER), Bangalore, and Tata Medical Center, Kolkata. Considering the large demography and increasing cancer mortality, India needs more trained psycho-oncologists to meet the greater demand in academic, research, and clinical practices. It is visible that psycho-oncological practices in the country lack scientific evidence based on coping, resilience, burden, post-traumatic growth, and spiritual approach. Developing psychometric standardized assessment tools based on socio-cultural and individual sensitivity could be the demands of the hours. Using measures beyond subjective self-reports and assessment over a longer time frame would be quality steps toward psycho-oncological research design. The psycho-oncological research also demands the explicit use of theoretical frameworks in designing the studies to the extent possible.

Psycho-oncological research involves multidisciplinary studies, which makes it difficult to integrate and access research from divergent sub-fields. Psycho-oncological research in India is visibly lacking with sufficient linkages between studies resulting in minimizing the quality of empirical studies. Psycho-oncology remains isolated and not well integrated with mainstream oncology in Indian clinical practices. Efforts need to be made to implement screening measures for significant distressing symptoms. Lack of awareness of the availability of psycho-oncological measures in Indian clinical settings has negatively affected tangible and valued outcomes such as compliance, overall functioning, and customer satisfaction. The practice and research in psycho-oncology depend on the availability of human resources rather than technological advancement. It is based on the ground realities with limited resources in the Indian clinical setting due to socio-cultural and psychological factors. Psychosocial distress is a major issue for the majority of the cancer-affected population, which requires immediate psychosocial assessment intervention.

9 798894 758664